I highly recommend Doug Hershey's book as a must-read. I call it a "primer." Doug answers questions most people are asking and does it simply, accurately, and articulately. This book, along with his CDs, is foundational teaching, like Israel 101! Doug is an excellent, interesting and anointed teacher.

—Bob Lichty
Apostolic leader in Youth With a Mission (YWAM) since 1971
(in Morocco, Spain, Portugal, Hawaii (U of N) and Virginia)

The silence in today's church over the subject of Israel is frightening, especially considering the times in which we are living. Doug's book, *The Christian's Biblical Guide to Understanding Israel*, shines a bright light on this topic and is helpful in revealing truth that is near and dear to God's heart.

—Jim Maher
Director, Israel Mandate, IHOP–KC

As a Jewish believer I see this book as something that is really needed. I like the way that it brings out the basic concepts that most of the body has clearly misunderstood or not been properly taught and presenting it in a way that is not too deep or overwhelming.

The last chapter was my favorite part of the book. It contained a prayer that tied everything together, but you cannot start here without reading the entire book first. It is a must-read and is a great reference.

If a believer does not understand the concepts that this book is presenting, then it is time to seek Him ever more. With a rise of anti-Semitism in the world, the last thing that we need is the body to turn her back on Israel, especially in these End Times.

Way to go, Doug!

—Roger Herman
Formerly of Branch of Israel

You will find this book of great use to begin a journey of learning about why Israel is such a large part of the heart of God. You'll gain a better appreciation of the plight of the Hebrew people and gain a better understanding the role of Israel in the End Time move of God. This really is a "must-have" book that can light a fire of greater passion for the kingdom of God and help you understand the people God calls "the apple of My eye."

—Kent Henry,
Worship Leader
President, Kent Henry Ministries, St. Louis, Missouri

This is a comprehensive, easy-to-read reference for Jew and Gentile alike. As a Jew and an Israeli, I learned a lot from this book myself. If I could name it, I would call it *Messiah for Dummies*.

—ADAM LEE ROSENFELD
www.adamandbethanyandco.com
The Pit That Became a Tower, Jerusalem, Israel

This book should be a bookmark in every Christian's Bible, stuck between Malachi and Matthew, so they could proceed informatively as to God's plan for Israel and the church. The tribe of Issachar had discerning of the times, and Esther had understanding of a moment in time. This book is both overdue reading for the church and yet imperative reading for world events that lie imminently ahead.

—JOHN WELSH,
Missions Pastor
New Life Church, Biddeford, Maine

The Christian's Biblical Guide to Understanding Israel is one of the most enjoyable books on Israel I have ever read! In just a few pages there is a clear and relevant picture of Israel's importance painted in a way that every follower of Jesus can understand. This guide will be an encouragement to every reader and a motivator to daily pray for the nation that God loves.

—JIM STERN,
Lead Pastor
Destiny Church, St. Louis, Missouri, www.destinychurch.org

The Christian's Biblical Guide to Understanding Israel provides an easy-to-read, insightful explanation of common misunderstandings concerning Israel, calling attention to the tender heart that God has for His people. Those with a heart for God are reminded to also have a heart for Israel. This book guides the reader to ponder and pray for the present-day issues in the land and for the people. I heartily recommend this book for those who wish to know more about Israel's place in God's master plan.

—JEFF POPE,
Associate Pastor
Little Country Church, Redding, California

The CHRISTIAN'S BIBLICAL GUIDE *to* UNDERSTANDING ISRAEL

DOUG HERSHEY

CREATION
HOUSE

THE CHRISTIAN'S BIBLICAL GUIDE TO UNDERSTANDING ISRAEL by
Doug Hershey
Published by Creation House Books
A Charisma Media Company
600 Rinehart Road
Lake Mary, Florida 32746
www.charismamedia.com

Unless otherwise noted, all Scripture quotations are from the New
American Standard Bible—Updated Edition, Copyright © 1960, 1962,
1963, 1968, 1971, 1972, 1973, 1975, 1977, 1995 by The Lockman
Foundation. Used by permission. (www.Lockman.org)

Scripture quotations marked NKJV are from the New King James
Version of the Bible. Copyright © 1979, 1980, 1982 by Thomas Nelson,
Inc., publishers. Used by permission.

Design Director: Bill Johnson
Cover design by M & N Marketing Group

Visit the author's website: www.EbedNetwork.com

Library of Congress Control Number: 2011923393
International Standard Book Number: 978-1-61638-477-7

First Edition

11 12 13 14 15 — 9 8 7 6 5 4 3 2 1
Printed in Canada

CONTENTS

FOREWORD

W E HAVE PEOPLE coming from many nations to be part of worship or prayer in "Succat Hallel," our 24/7 house of prayer overlooking Mt. Zion in Jerusalem. I recently was wishing I could find a concise, short book that would help introduce these intercessors to the Lord's heart for Israel.

I realized it needed to give a strong biblical foundation without getting bogged down in theological jargon and detail. It needed to give in short space a good understanding of issues, which could each be the subject of a thick book that most people would not take the time to read. It needed to speak to people who are open to investigate this subject and not just "preach to the choir" of those who already are convinced Israel and the Jewish people have not been "replaced" in God's heart or plans. It needed to create hunger to know more.

In Doug Hershey's *The Christian's Biblical Guide to Understanding Israel*, I have found this rare combination. This little gem is balanced, biblically sound, and yet not boringly academic, but strongly conveying the Lord's heart for Israel and the Jewish people.

I have lived in Jerusalem for almost ten years, have read extensively, and taught much on this subject. Yet I found I learned from Doug's teaching in this book. I have known Doug and his wife, Becky, for eleven years. They have been part of our team for on-site intercession and did an internship here with our house of prayer. I know they live the intercession they are encouraging for Israel.

Don't just read this book by yourself. Read it asking the Holy Spirit to breathe on all the Scripture it contains and causing them to come to life in you. Tell the Lord you really want to know Him better through knowing more of His heart. And get ready for a life-changing experience.

Grace and shalom.

—RICK RIDINGS,
founder/director Succat Hallel
(24/7 House of Prayer in Jerusalem)
www.jerusalempraise.com

Introduction

WHY CARE ABOUT ISRAEL?

Thus says the Lord of hosts, "I am exceedingly jealous for
Zion, yes, with great wrath I am jealous for her."
—ZECHARIAH 8:2

THIS BOOK STARTED out with titles like *Jealous for Zion* and *God's Heart for Israel.* As I started compiling my notes, though, I realized those titles were just too tame. To describe God's feelings toward Israel with such an overused and general word like "love" or to say Israel has a "special place in God's heart" not only does an injustice to the Almighty, but it is also a ridiculous understatement. It would be like calling Michelangelo's works in Rome's Sistine Chapel a "pretty good job of painting." Those who have actually been to the Sistine Chapel would stare with raised eyebrows at the silliness of such a comment. We do the same with simple phrases like "God loves Israel." Such a general phrase does not even begin to express the fullness of God's heart for Israel.

I am often asked by Christians, "So, what is the big deal with Israel? It's in the Bible, but what difference does it really make in my daily walk with Jesus?" My friend, if you have begun reading this book with questions such as these, you have taken the first step into reading the Bible through a whole new lens and getting to know a whole new side of Jesus. There is so much more here than you can realize.

There are two answers to these questions, both with equal relevance to our everyday walk with the Master. The first answer to why we should care about Israel today is simply because God does. If we truly love Him, we are bound to Him and want to know His heart, and then we will learn to love what He loves. There is a passion in the Lord's heart for Israel that is so deep and so pure that the word "love" fails to describe it. It involves His undying faithfulness to and everlasting compassion for Israel that we as Christians are now

1

a part of, as we will discover in the following pages. By the end of time, we will all thank Him and worship Him for including us (the Gentiles) in His undying compassion for Israel.

> He who touches you [Israel], touches the apple of His eye.
>
> —ZECHARIAH 2:8

The eye is a place on our bodies that has very little protection. The eyelid, a thin flap of skin, is all that protects the eye. There is little defense for intrusive objects. Even a small poke or speck of dust can become quite irritating or painful to the eye. It is a very tender place in the human body, just as Israel is a very tender place in the heart of God. He can become quite defensive when someone starts poking at Israel. If it is tender to Him, so it should be to us as well.

> For the LORD has chosen Zion; He has desired it for His habitation. This is My resting place forever; here I will dwell, for I have desired it.
>
> —PSALM 132:13–14

There is a specific place on Earth where the Lord loves to be. He has chosen not only a specific group of people but also a specific area of land for His purposes. He has desired it. If the Creator has desired something, shouldn't we, as His bride, be consumed by His desires to want to know what moves His heart too? Even while in the desert, the Lord said to Israel that He was taking them to "a land for which the LORD your God cares; the eyes of the LORD your God are always on it, from the beginning even to the end of the year" (Deut. 11:12). If we are to become like the Lord, we need to know why His eyes are always on this land and what we can do to join with Him in achieving His desires.

The second reason that understanding Israel is important for believers today is that her history holds special value for us that we will need in the turbulent days ahead. My hope is that this simple book will begin to prepare us for that time.

> Now these things happened to them [Israel in the desert] as an example, and they were written for our instruction, upon whom the ends of the ages have come.
>
> —1 CORINTHIANS 10:11

If we are living in the last days, as most Christians agree we are, there are specific lessons we can learn from Israel's history. What was the attitude of the Hebrew people in the desert? How did God deal with them? How does it relate to the church today, living in these troubled and tense times? According to Paul's exhortation here in 1 Corinthians 10, there are clear answers to these questions. Part of Israel's history was written to instruct future generations and lead us in the right way.

The church is starting to awaken to the reality of the days we are living in. In the last several years, it seems that there has been increased teaching on the last days, the Book of Revelation, and signs of the times. Who can deny the increase of natural disasters in the past ten to fifteen years? Some are even taking steps to physically prepare their homes and congregations by purchasing generators, starting food banks, or encouraging first-aid training for disaster situations. In certain locations, all of these will be needed. Yet I believe there are clear teachings and an understanding we are missing in our preparations.

It is time for the church to recognize the Jewish roots of our faith in a much broader way. This is not a call to force the Gentile church into Jewish customs or rituals, but rather to help the church find where she fits in the ultimate plan of the God of the universe. Israel is quickly becoming the central focus of God's plan for the earth and the nations of the world. Many Christians are starting to awaken to the fact that there is a "Christian/Israel connection," but we will soon see that this awakening will take on more practical aspects for the church as well. If the church continues to fail to recognize Israel's worth in God's unfolding plan, she will soon find herself behind the times and unprepared. We must gain a biblical and practical understanding of God's desires for Israel and the church, or in the days ahead many congregations will find themselves to be nothing more than a Sunday-morning book club. What happened to Israel in the desert was "written for our instruction" so we would know what to do and what to expect while living at the end of the age. God desires us to be prepared, and so far most churches have placed Israel on the back burner as just another church program or topic. Although God is gracious in allowing us to ignore the importance of His relationship with His people Israel, He will soon cause this to change.

Zechariah 14:4 says, "In that day His feet will stand on the Mount of Olives," describing a powerful arrival of the Jewish Messiah, or, for Christians, the second coming of Jesus. The very return of Jesus will be brought about by the nations of the earth gathering around Jerusalem to destroy her—Jesus returns in order to defend Israel. He will go forth and fight on Israel's behalf and strike down the people who have gone to war against Jerusalem (Zech. 14:12). He will then rule the earth from Jerusalem, and all nations will be required to come to worship Him (Zech. 14:16–17). The Lord is returning to judge the enemies of Israel and to bring us to Himself at the same time. There is certainly much more to the return of Jesus, but those who truly have a heart for Israel are much better prepared to recognize the signs of His coming.

Israel is very important to present-day believers in the Lord Jesus because the God of our Messiah is also the God of Israel. It could be suggested that when one becomes a Christian, one reads a Jewish book written by Jewish authors about a Jewish God who sends a Jewish Messiah, Jesus. Although salvation is through faith alone, without a basic understanding of God's love and desire for Israel, it is difficult to gain a true understanding of who the Lord really is. The more we comprehend the Lord's relationship with Israel, the more we are able to truly understand His covenant faithfulness, trust Him in difficult times, and bask in His everlasting love.

It can be said that Israel functions as God's barometer and time clock for the earth. At times, blessings and curses from God are often a direct reflection of how we treat and relate to Israel. This is especially true for the nations, as can been seen throughout history as well as today. How the church relates to Israel will play a greater and greater role in the coming days. The church must come to recognize her role or she will find herself struggling and confused.

According to Scripture, present-day Israel is about to embark on some of her most difficult and yet glorious days ever. We, as Christians, must not look the other way and continue as if nothing is happening, especially when we have clear instructions to practically minister to Israel:

> If the Gentiles have shared in their spiritual things, they are indebted to minister to them also in material things.
> —ROMANS 15:27

If we love Jesus and have been changed by the God of Israel, then it is our biblical responsibility to care for Israel in material and practical ways. How much more will this be true in the difficult days that lie ahead?

The chapters in this book cover a lot of topics with the intent to give the Christian reader a broad yet biblically detailed understanding of Israel. As you read the following pages, my prayer is that you would not only grow in knowledge but also gain an inner revelation of our historic role as End Time believers in relationship to God's people Israel and to learn to exercise that role in practical ways. While there is a great deal that can be learned regarding the relationship of the church to Israel and the Jewish people, even those with a mustard seed of faith can begin to see the dramatic events that are taking place throughout the world and how they relate to Israel and the church. My prayer is that through the pages of this book, you will begin to identify with God's love for His people and come to understand the role of the believer in relationship to Israel in these End times.

PART I

COMMONLY MISUNDERSTOOD CONCEPTS ABOUT ISRAEL

Chapter 1

THE CHOSEN PEOPLE

Lots of questions come up when Christians hear that the Jews are God's chosen people. What does "chosen" mean? Are they more important in God's eyes? Do they have special privileges that others don't? Do Jews get a free ride to heaven because God has chosen them? I have even watched Jews arrogantly puff out their chests, proclaiming that they are part of the chosen people of God, as if it was an elite club. The Bible paints a different picture in regard to these questions.

Most of the confusion comes from a misunderstanding of the word *chosen*. In the Western mind, the word *chosen* is equal to *preferred*. When playground kids pick teams, the choosing is based on who are the biggest, the fastest, and the strongest. When you go out for ice cream, you choose the flavors that you like best. When we choose something, it often means we prefer that thing to another.

When God chooses someone or a particular group, it is not only chosen for His benefit but to accomplish something much greater. God has a much greater plan, which is to demonstrate His character through His chosen vessel—in this case, the nation of Israel. He has chosen Israel not because they are the best suited for His plans, but because of His faithfulness and His love for His creation.

> For you are a holy people to the LORD your God; the LORD your God has chosen you to be a people for His own possession out of all the peoples who are on the face of the earth.
>
> —DEUTERONOMY 7:6

Most "chosen people" quotes stop right here. Of all the peoples of the earth, God has called Israel (and therefore the Jews as a people) "holy" and "a special treasure above all." At first glance, one would think that they must be the biggest and the strongest since God prefers them. But let's keep reading:

> The LORD did not set His love on you nor choose you because
> you were more in number than any of the peoples, for you were
> the fewest of all peoples, but because the LORD loved you and
> kept the oath which He swore to your forefathers, the LORD
> brought you out by a mighty hand and redeemed you from the
> house of slavery, from the hand of Pharaoh king of Egypt.
>
> —DEUTERONOMY 7:7–8

We can see from this passage that God chose Israel not because they were the biggest or the cream of the crop but because of His love for them as a people, His faithfulness to their forefathers, and as a demonstration of His might. From this, we see that God keeps His promises to men, even after hundreds and thousands of years have passed.

The Bible teaches us that Israel was chosen for a purpose. In Deuteronomy we read that Moses was preparing Israel to go into the land promised to Abraham, Isaac, and Jacob. For forty years, Israel was tested in the desert while God dwelled among them, making them ready. Israel had received the Law. They were obeying the Lord and were growing as a chosen people. Yet if there was one thing that Moses had learned about Israel, it was how easily they became arrogant and proud. Before they could begin to experience their God-given victories in the land, Moses needed to remind them to be on guard against their pride:

> Do not say in your heart when the LORD your God has driven
> them out before you, "Because of my righteousness the LORD
> has brought me in to possess this land," but it is because of the
> wickedness of these nations that the LORD is dispossessing them
> before you. It is not for your righteousness or for the uprightness
> of your heart that you are going to possess their land, but it is
> because of the wickedness of these nations that the LORD your
> God is driving them out before you, in order to confirm the oath
> which the LORD swore to your fathers, to Abraham, Isaac and
> Jacob. Know, then, it is not because of your righteousness that
> the LORD your God is giving you this good land to possess, for
> you are a stubborn people.
>
> —DEUTERONOMY 9:4–6

Israel was not chosen by God because they were the most righteous before Him. Here they are being warned before their very first battle that they were not even to consider such an idea. Israel was no better than the nations already living in the land. God was using Israel to judge the other nations' wickedness. Moses tells them three times in these verses, "It is not because of your righteousness," adding at the end, "You are a stubborn people"! In other words, God is telling Israel: "Don't get arrogant when I use you to bring about My purposes and uphold My faithfulness to your forefathers."

That was the first time Israel entered the Promised Land, during the time of Moses and Joshua. In Ezekiel we see a similar word spoken to Israel about the time that they entered the Promised Land for a second time. Ezekiel prophesied that God would scatter Israel to the four corners of the earth but would again return them to this very same piece of land:

> Therefore say to the house of Israel, "Thus says the Lord God, 'It is not for your sake, O house of Israel, that I am about to act, but for My holy name, which you have profaned among the nations where you went. I will vindicate the holiness of My great name which has been profaned among the nations, which you have profaned in their midst. Then the nations will know that I am the Lord,' declares the Lord God, 'when I prove Myself holy among you in their sight. For I will take you from the nations, gather you from all the lands and bring you into your own land.'"
> —Ezekiel 36:22–24

God tells Israel, "When I bring you back, it is not because you are perfect and holy, but because I will prove Myself holy among you in the sight of all the nations." Even though Israel was scattered to the nations, had profaned His name, and had endured the scorn of being rejected from the land of Israel, God is still faithful to Israel—not because they were anyone special, but because He was special in their midst. God will prove to all the nations of the earth that He is God. He has chosen Israel for such a task.

It could be said that God chose the nation of Israel in spite of themselves, or because they were a small nation of arrogant, stiff-necked people who constantly turned from the Lord. Nevertheless, it was through this family that the Creator chose to reveal Himself and His Son to the world. This teaches us that if He can show His glory and His loving characteristics through such a people, then there is still hope for our arrogant hearts and our wayward world.

The Bible teaches us that in the end, the Almighty will have taken this stiff-necked nation of Israel, changed her heart, and dwelled in her midst again. God will prove Himself faithful and holy in the sight of all the nations, just as Ezekiel said. If we are believers in the Lord Jesus, He will take our hard hearts and do the same in us for all to see. He has chosen Israel for a purpose: to reveal His power, His faithfulness, and His loving-kindness to all the nations of the earth. We who are believers in the Lord Jesus are joined with Israel in the same "olive tree" (Rom. 11:17) and have been chosen by God for the same purpose.

Chapter 2

BLESSINGS and CURSES

How we treat or respond to the nation of Israel is of the utmost importance to God. This is not just because of how He feels about Israel, but because our response to Israel directly affects His relationship with us. Throughout Scripture we are told that we will be measured the same way we measure others. If we judge others, we will be judged. Treat others the way you want to be treated. Show mercy to receive mercy. This is the justice of God. Yet there is something that God speaks to Abram and his family that is more intense than any of these biblical truths:

> And I will bless those who bless you, and the one who curses you
> I will curse.
>
> —Genesis 12:3

This verse is repeated in Genesis 27:29 as Isaac's blessing over Jacob (who became Israel) and in Numbers 24:9 as Balaam spoke over Israel. It is interesting to note that Balaam was being paid to speak a curse over Israel, but he would not do it. He understood the seriousness of being blessed or cursed by God based on his response to the nation of Israel.

What could have been so dire that Balaam would have turned down a house full of silver and gold rather than speak something contrary to God's Word? (See Numbers 24:13.) After all, it's just words, right?

For starters, Balaam knew that God meant every word He said. This is something that we miss in the English translation of the original Hebrew language.

> And I will *bless* those who *bless* you, and the one who *curses* you
> I will *curse*.
>
> —Genesis 12:3, emphasis added

The Hebrew word for "bless" used here is *barach*, and it is used twice in the same sentence. According to *Strong's Concordance*, the root of this word means "to kneel or to bend the knee, as in presenting a gift." It is often used to describe the results of divine favor or the prosperity of God on someone's life. A good example of this blessing was seen in Egypt, as the nation honored Joseph's God-given gifts and insight. Everything Joseph did prospered because of God's favor, which was obvious even to the Egyptians. Because Egypt blessed Joseph (the son of Israel), the people of Egypt were blessed. After the seven years of plenty, when the drought came, the Egyptians were prepared and were used to bless other peoples and nations. Genesis 12:3 states that God will honor or give divine favor and prosperity to those who give the same honor and value to Israel.

While there is one word used twice in this verse for *bless*, there are two different Hebrew words used for the word *curse*. The first Hebrew word is *qah-lal*. *Qah-lal* means "to be slight or to be light" (as in a material that is lacking or not strong or sturdy, or, to be slight, to be of little account or to take lightly). It carries the sense that in cursing someone, all you need to do is ignore, belittle, or despise them. It is ironic that today we view curses as certain four-letter words. No one would dare speak a curse word in church, yet many ignore, make light of, and belittle others on Sundays without a second thought. By doing so, many are demonstrating a biblical form of cursing without realizing what they are saying.

The second word used for *curse* is *ah-rar*. It is a very strong and harsh word that means "to abhor or detest" and has a root word that means "to spit." If something is *ah-rar*, or cursed, you cannot stand to be around it; it is unbearable, and you have an extreme and intense aversion to it. There is no middle ground with this word. *Ah-rar* is the word used in Genesis 3:14 when God speaks to the serpent and says, "Cursed [*ah-rar*] are you more than all cattle, and more than every beast of the field." *Ah-rar* describes the worst of the worst.

A clearer understanding of these two words for "curse" reads like this: "And the one who curses [*qah-lal*] you I will curse [*ah-rar*]" (Gen. 12:3). This verse literally means that the one who takes Israel lightly and refers to her as unimportant or worthless, God will detest and have an intense dislike for them—enough to spit them out of His mouth. Because of God's use of *ah-rar* in the Garden of Eden toward the serpent in Genesis 3:14 and 17, you could say that God will detest you in the same way He detests the devil if you despise and belittle Israel and that He will spit you out of His mouth. Balaam was right; an entire house full of silver and gold isn't worth that!

Belittling Israel is something God takes very personally. He has chosen this nation to demonstrate His character and personality to the world. When we slight Israel, we are slighting God's personal choice and despising His character. This is not unlike what the serpent told Eve at the tree: "Go ahead—eat the fruit. God didn't mean what He said. It's not that big of a deal." The serpent made God's words to be of little account and encouraged Eve to take Him lightly. God responded by cursing the serpent more than anything else on the earth because of it. Israel is the apple of God's eye. He doesn't respond kindly to anyone throwing dirt or belittling His choice of Israel.

It is interesting to look at the nations that have despised Israel and how God responded to them. Every Arab nation that has attacked Israel has continued to crumble and struggle, while Israel flourishes just on the other side of their borders. With the element of surprise, superior weapons, and overwhelming numbers, Arab nations still could not overtake Israel in the last sixty years of her existence. During Israel's war for independence, there is documentation from Arab soldiers claiming spiritual visions and seeing angels defending small bands of Israeli soldiers. Truly, God has been Israel's fortress and deliverer.

It could be said that the fall of the British Empire was a direct result of her betrayal of Israel during World War II. In the 1940s, it was said that the sun never set on the British Empire. But soon after England turned on Israel by supplying arms to her enemies and turning away boatloads of Jewish immigrants who were then returned to the Nazi-controlled nations, their empire started to crumble. Within fifty short years, the British Empire went from a worldwide superpower to a small island with increasing internal problems.

Some historians point to the Jewish nation as the catalyst in the fall of the Roman Empire. The amount of time, the effort, and the loss of men that occurred as the Romans tried to crush the final Jewish revolts were astounding. It was so dramatic that it stirred and encouraged other uprisings throughout the empire. In the coming years, these other revolts were too much to control, and the ancient superpower eventually gave way.

So, should we support every action of the Israeli government today so as to avoid the curse of God? As stated in the last chapter, Israel does not have a free pass with God, as history proves. It is not because of their righteousness that Israel is growing and prospering, but because of God's covenant faithfulness and His love for all people. When we bless Israel, we are honoring and esteeming the value and destiny of the nation chosen by God. By doing so, we are honoring and adoring the wisdom and the plan of God for choosing her to reveal Himself to the world. Israel is not perfect, nor should we pretend that she is. There have been many sins and injustices committed by the present-day nation. Israel has had good and bad leaders, just as in Old Testament times. And yet, through all of this, God has not rejected or turned His back on Israel, and neither should Christians. The fact remains that He has a plan to reveal His glory through Israel, one that began with Abraham, Isaac, and Jacob.

Thousands of years after Abraham, God has not changed, and neither have His promises to him. God is a faithful, covenant-keeping God. The Word of the Lord is as true today as it was when He spoke it to Abraham and his family:

> And I will bless those who bless you, and the one who curses you
> I will curse.
>
> —GENESIS 12:3

In other words, God will kneel and present gifts to those who kneel and present gifts to Israel, and He will spit upon those who despise and brush aside Israel as insignificant.

Chapter 3

PEACE

Peace—what a rich word in regards to Israel! Peace has always been the focus of the world when looking at today's Israel and the complex tensions that exist between her and her neighbors. When considering the current political situation in the region, we tend to use our interpretation of peace as the goal rather than that of the Bible. Although there may not appear to be any peace, as is often the case with God, He is more concerned with our true self, which is internal, rather than that which can be seen, which is external. If we clean the inside, then the outside will also be clean (Matt. 23:26). Such is the case with peace.

Many are familiar with the Hebrew word for peace, which is shalom, yet few really understand what it means. The obvious definition of peace that most have is the absence of conflict or the opposite of war. If people are not fighting, then there is peace. Although there is truth to this, it is only one aspect of the word *shalom*, which is in reality a many-faceted diamond.

Shalom literally means "well-being and health, to be well, content and in a friendly state." It speaks of health and prosperity. Furthermore, *shalom* is taken from the root word *shalam*, which means "to be safe in mind, body, or estate." It speaks of completeness, fullness, or a type of wholeness that encourages you to give back—to generously repay something in some way.

True biblical *shalom* refers to an inward sense of completeness or wholeness. Although it can describe the absence of war, a majority of biblical references refer to an inner completeness and tranquility. If this is the kind of peace that you make with your enemies, then they are no longer your enemies but friends whom you desire to prosper. In Israel today, when you greet someone or say good-bye, you say, "Shalom." You are literally saying, "May you be full of well-being" or "May health and prosperity be upon you."

If this is the way we understand biblical peace, then suddenly many verses take on a whole new meaning. With this Hebrew thought of shalom in mind, let's look at a few scriptures about peace:

> Speak to Aaron and to his sons, saying, "Thus you shall bless the sons of Israel. You shall say to them: The LORD bless you, and keep you; the LORD make His face shine on you, and be gracious to you; the LORD lift up His countenance on you, and give you *peace.*"
>
> —NUMBERS 6:23–26, EMPHASIS ADDED

These verses are well known by both Jews and Christians. What is ironic is that God told Aaron to bless Israel with peace while they were getting ready to conquer the Promised Land. If peace means the absence of war, then this doesn't make sense, since they would soon be destroying cities. What God was referring to was an inner peace and completeness brought on by sharing in His countenance and His protection. That was the blessing that Israel needed! Israel was to rarely experience times of outward peace, but even in the midst of battle, they were to have an inward rest brought on by the presence of the Lord, regardless of the outward circumstances. So it should be for us as well.

> Pray for the peace of Jerusalem: "May they prosper who love you. May *peace* be within your walls, and prosperity within your palaces."
>
> —PSALM 122:6–7, EMPHASIS ADDED

These days, many are starting to pray for the peace of Jerusalem due to the rising threat from Israel's enemies. However, I would suggest to you that this exhortation to pray is not so Israel can live without conflict. It is so that Jerusalem can fulfill its destiny as set by the only One who can bring complete restoration to the city that Jesus referred to as "the city of the great King."

I believe Psalm 122:6–7 should serve as a prayer for Israel's spiritual revival. Verse 7 says that we are praying for peace *within* Jerusalem's walls and palaces. That is where true biblical peace is found: within. Pray for the fullness and completeness of Jerusalem. Pray that there may be such wholeness and safety found in her palaces that she willingly gives and rewards others with that peace. From this perspective, it almost sounds like we are praying for the return of Israel's Messiah, the Prince of Peace, to establish His throne in Jerusalem.

> And suddenly there appeared with the angel a multitude of the heavenly host praising God and saying, "Glory to God in the highest, and on earth peace among men with whom He is pleased."
> —LUKE 2:13–14, EMPHASIS ADDED

In this passage a vast quantity of angels has appeared to celebrate the birth of Jesus. This is a very common Christmas verse, but do not allow yourself to become indifferent to what is actually happening. The angels are in fact rejoicing and celebrating the amazing fulfillment of Isaiah 9:6: "For a child will be born to us, a son will be given to us…His name will be called…Prince of *peace*" (emphasis added). The Prince of Peace has been born!

With the full understanding and realization of what is happening, who in heaven could miss this event? A great host of angels appeared to proclaim, "Glory to God in the highest!" This is the utmost way to offer praise and glory in the Bible. There are several places in Scripture that proclaim glory to God, but only one other place in which this degree of glory is given, and that is also in reference to Jesus. In Luke 19:38, Jesus is welcomed to Jerusalem with praises of, "Peace in heaven and glory in the highest!" When the angels proclaim this in Luke 2:13, there can be no mistake to whom they are speaking. Not just glory to God, but glory to God in the *highest*. To the God who is in the very highest place above all things everywhere: there is none whom compares to You, and You are the sole recipient of all glory and praise for what You have done! That is what the angels are proclaiming.

They are proclaiming this because of the birth of Jesus, the Prince of Peace. Jesus is the ultimate Prince of fullness, safety, and wholeness, whom the angels have known and worshiped in heaven since before the beginning of time. To the astonishment of all of heaven, He has just been born on Earth as a man. Literally, the angels are praising God and saying, "The promised Messiah has come! Glory to God who is in the highest place! The Prince of Peace, whom we have worshiped in heaven since before the ages began, is now alive on Earth! Finally, a rest, a fullness, and a completeness is now among the men that the Father so passionately loves!" The birth of Jesus didn't bring peace to the earth; He *is* the true Peace who came to the earth.

> Blessed are the peacemakers, for they shall be called sons of God.
> —MATTHEW 5:9

Hopefully by now, you are catching the full meaning of a biblical peace. In this verse, Jesus is not referring to mediators or political negotiators, but to those who carry an inward sense of the fullness and safety that is only available through sonship with God. In the Hebrew understanding of *shalom*, there is a point at which you have so much *shalom* that it spills out from you and is repaid or rendered to others. And so, as you make others peaceful and inwardly complete, that makes you a peacemaker. Jesus said these peacemakers will be called sons of God, and Jesus was called the Son of God. By sharing God's uncontainable peace with others, we become just like Jesus. It is as simple as that. With this understanding of Matthew 5:9, it fits the other "blessed" verses around it much more completely.

There are many other examples worthy of study regarding *shalom*. Peace is so much more than the world's one-sided definition. We must find our understanding of it through the Bible and from the God of Israel. We will need it in the days ahead.

> The LORD bless you from Zion, and may you see the prosperity of Jerusalem all the days of your life. Indeed, may you see your children's children. *Peace be upon Israel!*
> —PSALM 128:5–6, EMPHASIS ADDED

Chapter 4

JESUS and the LAW

A s a Gentile with a heart for Israel, this was one of the most diffi-cult chapters for me to write, not because of the topic but because of vast misunderstanding of how the church today views Torah, or the Law of Moses. Torah means "teaching" or "instruction," not "law," as many believe. This fact is one often lost in our English translations.

The Hebrew view of Torah is that it is God's instruction received at Mt. Sinai, recorded by Moses in Genesis to Deuteronomy, and encompassing every aspect of life. The emphasis on the writings of Moses were so that Israel could live the kind of lives that God wanted them to live, rather than a set of policed rules from God. For this reason, I will avoid referring to the five books of Moses as Law and use "God's instructions" or "the writings of Moses." This will enhance your understanding as we consider how Jesus fulfilled all things.

To be clear, this chapter is not intended to restrict a Christian's freedom in Jesus, instill regulations in the church, or reinstitute what Paul refers to as the "ministry of death and condemnation." (See 2 Corinthians 3:7, 9.) This chapter is intended to introduce how Jesus related to the writings of Moses. The more we understand the Old Testament, the more we can see the entire Bible as one book being the complete revelation of Jesus. Derek Prince, a renowned Bible teacher, said it like this: "You cannot fully understand the Bible, unless you know something about Israel. And if you are confused about Israel, you are confused about the Bible."[1]

A closer look at the words and actions of Jesus will reveal that He never spoke anything contrary to God's instructions to Moses or the prophets. The more we become acquainted with the Torah, the more this statement becomes clear. A large majority of the teachings of Jesus were given either during the annual feasts found in Leviticus or were practical explanations on how to apply God's instructions at Sinai on a personal level. As He said Himself, Jesus never intended to replace anything but to become the key that would unlock everything:

> Do not think that I came to abolish the Law or the Prophets; I did not come to abolish but to fulfill. For truly I say to you, until heaven and earth pass away, not the smallest letter or stroke shall pass from the Law until all is accomplished.
>
> —MATTHEW 5:17–18

To fully understand what the Lord is saying here, we need to understand two words that are used: *abolish* and *fulfill*. In the original language, *abolish* means "to loosen down, as to disintegrate or to destroy." Whether it was a slow disintegration or a quick destruction, the result of something being abolished was the disappearance of that something forever. *Fulfill* means "to abundantly supply or provide for, or to fill a vessel to the brim." According to this word, if you truly have fulfilled a contract, that means that the terms were met to the fullest extent possible with nothing left undone in any aspect.

In this verse, Jesus said His intention in coming was not to have God's instructions slowly disintegrate away to nothing or to quickly demolish it, but to abundantly provide for all that was required under the Torah. The picture here is that by His coming, the writings of Moses would be totally and completely satisfied in every aspect for generations to come, until Christ's return. The Torah was not to be discarded or replaced but to be looked at and marveled over with awe for God at how perfectly Jesus the Messiah fulfilled everything. Quite simply, Jesus said the Torah would prove that He is the Messiah.

Throughout His teachings, Jesus often pointed to the five books of Moses as proof of who He was. Jesus said He was like the serpent that Moses lifted up in the desert (John 3:14). He said He was the manna who fell from heaven in the desert (John 6:50). At Passover, He equated His blood with the blood of the Passover lamb, which was the blood of the covenant (Matt. 26:28). In John 12:48–50, Jesus publicly spoke of Himself in the same way Moses said the coming Prophet would speak. (See Deuteronomy 18:18–19.) At the time, many Pharisees and elders of Israel prided themselves in their studies of the Torah. It was their responsibility to teach God's instructions, and yet Jesus said they were missing the most important part:

> You search the Scriptures because you think that in them you will have eternal life; and *it is these that bear witness about Me....* For if you believed Moses, you would believe Me; *for he*

wrote about Me. But if you do not believe his writings, how will you believe My words?

—JOHN 5:39, 46–47, EMPHASIS ADDED

Jesus is saying that if we do not recognize Him in the writings of Moses, how can we really come to know and understand the fullness and purpose of His coming? Jesus didn't just show up in Israel after thousands of years of quietly watching from above. Almost everything about Him was prophesied or spoken of ahead of time, starting in the Garden of Eden until He was born in Bethlehem. In fact, many times in the Old Testament, God appeared in the form of man, interacted with men, and yet spoke as God. We see examples of this in Genesis 18 as the Lord appears as Abraham's guest and speaks to Sarah about a son. In Genesis 32 He appears and wrestles with Jacob and changes his name to Israel. In Joshua 5–6 He appears to Joshua as the captain of the Lord's host and tells Joshua the battle plan for Jericho. These "appearances" are found throughout the Old Testament. Could this "man/God" be Jesus?

Even after Jesus was resurrected, He continued to point to the scriptures to prove who He was and why the recent events had to happen the way they did. Without recognizing Him, two discouraged disciples met Jesus on the road to Emmaus and experienced one of the most revelatory teachings that Jesus ever spoke concerning Himself:

> And beginning with Moses and with all the prophets, He [Jesus] explained to them the things concerning Himself in all the Scriptures.
>
> —LUKE 24:27

I would like to get that teaching CD! Jesus, the resurrected Lord, was teaching about Jesus the Promised Messiah from Jesus the Word of God! I wonder how long that took to explain, since Jesus can be found in every book from Genesis to Malachi. Jesus is everywhere in the Old Testament.

Apparently, Paul and the first-century church got that teaching CD. The act of witnessing, for Paul, often stated that he was trained in the Torah from his childhood. Today, our evangelism is often based on our experiences or on a few New Testament verses. For Paul, the Torah was more than enough to teach for weeks. For Paul, trusting in Jesus the risen Christ was not an issue of simply believing some spiritual ideas—it was an issue of believing solid biblical fact:

23

> And according to Paul's custom, he went to them, and for three Sabbaths reasoned with them from the Scriptures, explaining and giving evidence that the Christ had to suffer and rise again from the dead, and saying, "This Jesus whom I am proclaiming to you is the Christ."
>
> —Acts 17:2–3

Just like the Lord, when the apostles would teach, they would do so from what we today call the Old Testament to prove and give evidence that Jesus was the promised Messiah. This was all they had; it was all they needed. Since the New Testament canon was formed long after the time of the apostles, the scriptures from which they taught and gained life-giving wisdom and supernatural power was from what we call the Old Testament. It is ironic that many churches today pray for the power and the life of the first-century church and yet often disregard large portions of the Torah that the first-century brethren depended on. The proof and evidence that this Jesus whom the apostles followed was really the Messiah is found in the Torah.

> "Teacher, which is the great commandment in the Law?" And He said to him, "You shall love the Lord your God with all your heart, and with all your soul, and with all your mind."
>
> —Matthew 22:36–37

Of the 613 instructions found in the Torah, what was God's single-most intention for Israel? If we could boil down five books of Moses to one main point, what would it be? It is a fair question and is still discussed by Jews today. Jesus said that the whole point of the Torah and all of the prophets' messages was to have us fall deeper and deeper in love with God in every aspect of our being. If that is still true today, how can we as Christians disregard something that was intended to point us to the depths of loving Jesus, especially when Jesus said that Moses wrote about Him?

God is starting to revive a love for the Old Testament in His church and is proving to us that the Bible really is one complete revelation, not two completely separate testaments. Through the eyes of the Holy Spirit, I pray that you find these same depths of wholly devoted love in your heart, soul, and mind that Jesus spoke of as you read the writings of Moses.

Chapter 5

HAS GOD REJECTED ISRAEL?

R EPLACEMENT THEOLOGY IS one of the most detrimental and diabolical seeds of distrust toward God's faithfulness ever planted in the mind of man. It is difficult to find a one-hundred-year span in the last eighteen to nineteen hundred years where this false doctrine has not fueled Christian persecution of the Jewish people or adversely affected the heart and mind of the church. Furthermore, both the Old and New Testaments warn against the complete rejection of the Jewish people. I believe it is one of the worst lies the church has ever believed in the last two thousand years.

The basis of replacement theology is that God has rejected Israel and "replaced" her with the church. Because of Israel's unfaithfulness, her constant spiritual adultery, and her outright rejection of Jesus the Messiah, the belief is that God has started over in this age of grace with the church as His new covenant and chosen people. While the church goes on to receive all of the blessings and rewards of the Lord, the Jews are now left with the covenant curses found in Deuteronomy 28.

The early beginnings of this "doctrine" entered the early church in a rather unassuming way. For its first fifteen years of existence, Christianity was exclusively Jewish and was known as a sect of Judaism. In Acts 15 (circa A.D. 49), a council is called in Jerusalem to discuss what to do with the Gentiles who were now being saved and filled with the Holy Spirit. The result of the council was a clear decision in Acts 15:28 that "seemed good to the Holy Spirit and to us [the apostles]" not to hinder the Gentiles that were coming to the Lord by requiring them to obey God's instructions at Sinai. This moment would forever change the life of the church.

Instead of the church becoming "one new man," the joining of Jew and Gentile as God intended and as Ephesians 2:11–22 speaks of, bitterness over differences drove them apart. Over time it became inevitable that Gentile believers, who had no real understanding of God's dealings with Israel, would outnumber the Jewish believers whose family and nation brought forth the Messiah. Within one generation following the death of the apostles, the majority of the church leadership consisted of Gentiles. What had been recognized as a sect of Judaism was now led by Gentiles who did not follow the Torah. This resulted in a growing tension and conflict between Jews and Gentiles in the early church, as well as within society as a whole.

By the early to mid-second century, many church leaders would start to point to current events to "prove" God's rejection of Israel. In their view, God's rejection of Israel was obvious. The Romans ransacked the temple, the focus of all Jewish life, and the sacrificial system was ended in A.D. 70. The Romans continued to destroy pockets of Jewish resistance, burned Jewish cities, and forbid Jews to enter Jerusalem on pain of death. Some Christians even used the frustration exhibited by the apostle Paul when he declared that he was going to the Gentiles as proof of this turning away of God from His people. It was during the second and third centuries that the theme of "Christ-killers" was applied to the Jews in the writings of early church fathers, like Justin Martyr, a converted Gentile philosopher, as he spoke openly of Israel "justly suffering" for their sins. From his writings and those of other early church leaders like Origen, there is an obvious contempt toward Jews and the belief that God had completely rejected Israel as punishment for their having crucified Jesus.

Feeling that their arguments against the Jews were justified, the early church leaders turned their attention to the future. The pervading view was that the church was no longer a remnant of Israel but a completely separate Gentile entity. Although the scriptures were valued, it was thought that any clear connection with the Jewish scriptures (meaning the Old Testament) would give weight to Israel's importance. Giving validity to Israel's birthright did not fit the doctrine of the church, so a new view of the Old Testament was taught, one that could still teach biblical values and the numerous Old Testament prophecies of Jesus while ignoring the place of Israel in it. The answer was to view and teach the Old Testament as a parable or an allegory.

In an allegory or a parable, the characters and events are included solely as a means for relating a point and have no particular value in and of themselves. For example, any blessings spoken to Israel were now said to relate to the church, the Sabbath was now represented by Sunday, and so on. The result of this view of the Old Testament was that the Bible suddenly did not really mean what it seemed to be saying; it was now seen to be a fable—a story with hidden meanings. The interpretation of the Old Testament became completely subjective and open to anyone's understanding, thereby destroying the former value of its historical context and scriptural confirmation. The Word of God was no longer seen as something solid with clear-cut intentions but a collection of confusing books that very few could understand. This, unfortunately, is not unlike the way that many Christians interpret the Old Testament today. All of this Old Testament confusion was started by wanting to replace Israel with the church.

It must be stated that this has not been the view of the entire church since the time of the apostles, but of several popular Gentile church leaders in the early second, third, and fourth centuries like Justin Martyr, Origen, Jerome, and Augustine. Yet their influence and teachings can still be seen today in many churches and seminaries. This view that God has rejected the nation of Israel as "Christ-killers" has supported many dark years of church history, such as the Crusades, the Spanish Inquisition, and even the German church's inactivity during the early years of World War II. Today, much of the Christian confusion regarding the writings of Moses and the practicality of Bible stories can be traced to the allegorical style of teaching in Old Testament history. We must return to actually believing the Old Testament, understanding the promises God made to Israel (which includes those of us joined by faith), and trusting what the Word of God says.

So, what does the Bible say about God's anger and rejection of Israel? Has He really forsaken and broken the covenant He made with the Jewish nation? The scriptural answers to this could fill a book of its own and could become an incredible study. Here are some, for starters.

Leviticus 26:14–43 describes the terrible things that Israel will experience if they do not obey the Lord and instead reject His ways. Israel's sins would bring terrible sicknesses, cannibalism, destruction of cities and sanctuaries, weak and fearful hearts, and their being scattered to the land of their enemies, to name just a few. After all of this, we come to verse 44:

> Yet in spite of this, when they are in the land of their enemies, I
> will not reject them, nor will I so abhor them as to destroy them,
> breaking My covenant with them; for I am the LORD their God.
> But I will remember for them the covenant with their ancestors,

whom I brought out of the land of Egypt in the sight of the nations, that I might be their God. I am the LORD.

—LEVITICUS 26:44–45

Despite their degree of sin and because He is faithful, God was still willing to keep His covenant with Israel. The danger of replacement theology is that if Israel could reach a point where they and all of their descendants were rejected by God because of their sins, who's to say we and our families are not close to that point as well? We all have sinned, as have our families. If God has not remained faithful to Abraham, Isaac, and Jacob (who became Israel), then what hope do we have? This belief is a direct challenge to the faithfulness and the trustworthiness of the Creator.

Thus says the LORD, who gives the sun for light by day and the fixed order of the moon and the stars for light by night, who stirs up the sea so that its waves roar; The LORD of hosts is His name: "If this fixed order departs from before Me," declares the LORD, "then the offspring of Israel also will cease from being a nation before Me forever." Thus says the LORD, "If the heavens above can be measured and the foundations of the earth searched out below, then I will also cast off all the offspring of Israel for all that they have done," declares the LORD.

—JEREMIAH 31:35–37

Jeremiah asks, "Will God cast off Israel as a nation before Him?" The answer is, yes—once the sun stops rising, the moon and the stars stop shining, and when the heavens are measured. Then, yes, He will reject Israel for all they have done. The problem is, the sun came up today, and scientists still can't seem to find the edge of the universe. So for now, according to Jeremiah, that is proof that He still has not forsaken Israel.

Paul found himself confronting this arrogant doctrine as he wrote to the Romans in chapters 9–11, years before the temple was destroyed. Little did he know that the church would still be asking the same questions and need his answers two thousand years later!

I say then, *God has not rejected His people, has He? May it never be!* For I too am an Israelite, a descendant of Abraham, of the tribe of Benjamin. *God has not rejected His people whom He foreknew.*

—Romans 11:1–2, emphasis added

Paul's point is a sobering one today. If God has rejected Israel and all of the Jews, then God has also rejected Paul because he was an Israelite. If God only rejected the Jewish leaders who killed Jesus, this also would include Paul, since he was trained as a Pharisee from his childhood. Paul was saying that he and his ministry were proof that this nascent spreading doctrine that completely rejected all Jews and flattered the Gentiles was a lie. If God has rejected Israel, then a Jewish man who was under God's punishment wrote most of the New Testament and should be rejected completely.

As stated at the beginning of this chapter, this replacement theology that replaces Israel with the church has done vast damage to believers throughout the centuries, and the effects can still be seen today. Scripture is full of God's love and faithfulness toward His people Israel, even in the midst of their sin and wanderings. In a later chapter, a short look at Israel's present-day history and accomplishments will also prove this to be true. We as believers can rest and trust in the Lord's faithfulness to Israel. He has been faithful to them, and He will be faithful to us as well, as we are now a grafted-in part of the family of Israel.

> But Zion said, "The Lord has forsaken me, and the Lord has forgotten me." "Can a woman forget her nursing child and have no compassion on the son of her womb? Even these may forget, but *I will not forget you.* Behold, I have inscribed you on the palms of My hands; your walls are continually before Me."
>
> —Isaiah 49:14–16, emphasis added

PART II

THE BIBLICAL VIEW of GENTILE CHRISTIANS and JEWS

Chapter 6

BLESSINGS of the JEWS

GENESIS 15 IS one of the most pivotal times in the entire Bible. The God of all the earth appeared to a man, Abram, to make a covenant with him and his descendants forever. What happened that day stands as a spiritual plumb line, or compass, in the lives of all of Israel and those joined to her (the church), even up to our generation.

> Then He said to him, "I am the LORD, who brought you out of Ur of the Chaldeans, to give you this land to inherit it." And he said, "LORD God, how shall I know that I will inherit it?" So He said to him, "Bring Me a three-year-old heifer, a three-year-old female goat, a three-year-old ram, a turtledove, and a young pigeon." Then he brought all these to Him and cut them in two, down the middle, and placed each piece opposite the other; but he did not cut the birds in two.
>
> —GENESIS 15:7–10, NKJV

Abram understood what God was telling him to do. In the original Hebrew language, there is only one word for covenant: *b'reet*. It means literally "to cut the meat" to make a covenant. Those making the covenant would take a couple of animals and cut them in half, down the spine. The two parts of the animal were placed on either side of a natural trench or ditch, allowing the blood to pool together between the pieces. The two parties making the covenant would then walk through the blood and make a lifelong covenant that, if broken, would end in the loss of the life of the transgressor. This action was saying, "If I break this covenant, then it will be my blood that will be shed and you may walk through it. I give my life to uphold this covenant between you and me." Although extreme to modern minds, the Book of Hebrews echoes this sentiment:

> For where a covenant is, *there must of necessity be the death of the one who made it*. For a covenant is valid only when men are dead,

for it is never in force while the one who made it lives. Therefore even the first covenant was not inaugurated without blood.

—Hebrews 9:16–18, emphasis added

These covenants were so serious that most of the men of the Bible rarely ever made them. Of those men who did make covenants, most only made one in their lifetime. Four men of the Bible made two covenants, and only one man, David, made three. David's covenants were with God, with the nation of Israel to be their leader, and with Jonathan. (It could be said that David made six covenants, as David and Jonathan reaffirmed their covenant with each other three times.) Some of these men and their families faced dire consequences when they broke their covenants. This was more than a promise soon to be forgotten—this was a lifelong commitment sealed in blood.

For Abram, then, this was beginning to look like a no-win situation. Who can perfectly uphold a covenant with God? If he did not enter this covenant with God, he would have disobeyed God's instructions, and there would be no promise to Abram's descendants. If he did enter the covenant, Abram was placing the blood of his unborn children into a covenant that no man could keep. Despite the grim outlook, the answer was about to appear. The Lord seems to enjoy revealing Himself when it looks like there is no possible solution.

Like most Christians, for years I assumed that God the Father interacted with and appeared to men until Jesus was born as the only Son sent to save the world. Yet that can't be possible when we begin listening to the scriptures and to Jesus Himself. Here are just a couple verses that point to this:

No one has seen God at any time. The only begotten Son, who is in the bosom of the Father, He has declared Him.

—John 1:18, nkjv, emphasis added

Not that anyone has seen the Father, except the One who is from God; He has seen the Father.

—John 6:46, emphasis added

If no one has ever seen the Father, then who is appearing as the Lord in the form of a man and yet speaking as God? This God/man (whom I believe is Jesus Himself) can be seen physically "appearing" throughout the Old Testament to men like Abraham, Isaac, Jacob, Moses, Joshua, Gideon, and many, many others.

In Genesis 15:13–16, God calms Abram's fears by reassuring him that He will watch over his descendants, deliver them, and bring them back to the land He promised. As for Abram, he is assured of nothing but good days ahead and to be buried in peace. After the sun goes down, Jesus appears.

> And it came to pass, when the sun went down and it was dark, that behold, there appeared *a smoking oven* and *a burning torch* that passed between those pieces.
>
> —GENESIS 15:17, NKJV, EMPHASIS ADDED

Did you see Him? Did you recognize Him through the darkness? According to the original language, Abram saw two things pass between the pieces of flesh: a glowing furnace, or literally, bread oven, and a brightly burning torch. As many other Old and New Testament prophets after him realized, there is nothing on Earth that can compare to or describe the things seen and experienced in the heavenly realm. These were the two most appropriate earthly things that Abram could use to describe this sight.

It is interesting to compare what Abram saw with what other prophets saw in their experiences with the Lord. Hundreds of years after Abram lived, the prophet Ezekiel saw the heavens open and saw visions of God (Ezek. 1:1). Look at his description of what he saw:

> And on that which resembled a throne, high up, was a figure with *the appearance of a man.* Then I noticed from the appearance of His loins and upward *something like glowing metal* that looked like fire all around within it, and from the appearance of His loins and downward I saw *something like fire*; and there was a radiance around Him.
>
> —EZEKIEL 1:26–27, EMPHASIS ADDED

Thousands of years after Abram's encounter, John the apostle had a similar spiritual vision of his best friend Jesus. Note this brief passage in which John describes the glorified Jesus:

> His eyes were like *a flame of fire.* His feet were like *burnished bronze, when it has been made to glow in a furnace.*
>
> —REVELATION 1:14–15, EMPHASIS ADDED

Abram saw the Lord as a glowing oven and a flaming torch. Ezekiel described the appearance of this God/man as being like glowing metal and something like fire. John described the image of Jesus as a flame of fire and glowing bronze in a furnace. Even though thousands of years separate these three men, it appears that they were all looking at the same thing—or at the same Person. Hebrews 13:8 lends weight to this revelation, saying, "Jesus Christ is the same yesterday, today, and forever." There can be no doubt that this was Abram's first encounter with the Lord Jesus.

The Lord goes on to tell Abram something miraculous that affects Christians even today:

> I will establish My covenant between Me and you and your descen-
> dants after you throughout their generations for an everlasting cove-
> nant, to be God to you and to your descendants after you. I will give
> to you and to your descendants after you, the land of your sojourn-
> ings, all the land of Canaan, for an everlasting possession; and I
> will be their God.
>
> —GENESIS 17:7–8, EMPHASIS ADDED

The Lord Jesus makes it clear that He will be the one to establish, accomplish, and confirm this covenant not only with Abram but also with all of his descendants forever. This means that the total and complete success of the covenant would not depend on Abram but on God, and it would last until the end of time. In essence, what the Lord Jesus was saying was, "Abram, I promise to you that I will establish both sides of this covenant with you and your descendants forever. If you or any of your descendants break this covenant, I will pay the price in my own blood until the end of time."

Thousands of years after Abraham lived, Jesus shed His blood on the cross and died for the breaches in the covenant caused by Abraham's descendants and to satisfy the covenant that was made. At the cross, if the devil could kill and destroy Jesus or cause Him to renege on any aspect of His covenant with Abraham, then the covenant would be over. God's Word would be invalid, and the world would be completely and totally in the hands of Satan. Jesus then rose from the dead to eternally establish the covenant that would not end with His death but continue forever.

The Book of Romans clearly states that through the sacrifice of Jesus, Christians are children of Abraham, or Abraham's descendants. (See Romans

4.) As children of Abraham, we are now a part of this covenant. The blood of this covenant covers our sins and transgressions, as well as all those who repent of their sins and come to Him. This is not a promise of deliverance solely to the Jewish people but to all who come to Him in faith, as Abraham did. God's plan was to bring us, the Gentile church, into this everlasting covenant, together with Abraham's descendants. This is why there is such power in the blood of Jesus.

The Lord's everlasting covenant promise was to bring Abraham's descendants back to the land that God promised him to possess forever and to restore their relationship with God. He would be their God, and they would be His people. Jesus Himself now upholds this covenant forever and proclaims, "[I am] the *living One*; and *I was dead*, and behold, *I am alive forevermore*, and I have the keys of death and of Hades (Rev. 1:18, emphasis added). Anyone who comes to Him in faith as Abraham did enters into this blood covenant.

The devil's plan has always been to destroy God's blood covenant with man. He could do it in one of three different ways: (1) Kill one man, Jesus—a partner in the covenant; (2) kill Abraham's descendants—the second partner in the covenant; or (3) destroy and divide the promised land of Canaan. The devil first tried his best to kill Jesus. Since Jesus could not be destroyed, then he figured perhaps Abraham's descendants could be. This is why the Jews have been persecuted throughout history like no other people or nation on the earth. They have a covenant with God. This has been the root cause behind the diabolical efforts focused against them by many of the world's leaders throughout the last two thousand years, even up to today. For us as Christians, such threats should be seen as an attack on our own family and on the God in whom we trust. If the devil can't destroy all of the Jewish people, then perhaps he can make sure that the land of Israel is never fully possessed by them.

This is the spiritual motive behind many of today's political headlines. This covenant is also the root spiritual issue that will bring the nations of the world to fight against Jerusalem and cause the return of Jesus. By His coming, He will once and for all secure every aspect of this covenant forever!

In John 8, Jesus spoke of Abraham's joy at seeing the Lord:

> "Your father Abraham rejoiced to see My day, and he saw it and was glad." So the Jews said to Him, "You are not yet fifty years old,

and have You seen Abraham?" Jesus said to them, "Truly, truly, I
say to you, before Abraham was born, I am."

—JOHN 8:56–58

The Jews found it incredibly offensive, yet His words were filled with pro-
found truth. The words of Jesus to the Jewish leaders held more weight than
anyone could have realized.

Chapter 7

CHRISTIANS GRAFTED IN

THE TERM "GRAFTED in" has become increasingly popular in the church today among Christians who support Israel. It is a phrase that speaks of how Christians have become a part of the spiritual nation of Israel. As Paul wrote to the Gentile Roman church about being grafted in, everyone understood the metaphor he used. Yet over the centuries, the concept of grafting, especially as it relates to the olive industry, has become largely unknown to our Western culture. Through this metaphor, a rich and beautiful understanding can be seen regarding why God grafted the Gentiles into a Jewish tree:

> And you [Gentiles], being a wild olive, were *grafted in* among them [Israel] and became partaker with them of the rich root of the olive tree, do not be arrogant toward the branches; but if you are arrogant, remember that it is not you who supports the root, but the root supports you. You will say then, "Branches were broken off so that I might be grafted in." Quite right, they were broken off for their unbelief, but you stand by your faith. Do not be conceited, but fear; for if God did not spare the natural branches, He will not spare you, either.
> —ROMANS 11:17–21, EMPHASIS ADDED

In these verses Paul compares Israel to an olive tree. Olive trees have some very unique characteristics. They prefer a soil rich in limestone, a humid coastal climate, and have no trouble growing on rocky slopes and rough terrain. Olive trees also have a remarkably strong and vast root system and can survive in drought conditions. This extensive root system also gives life to the tree and adds to its amazing longevity, reaching hundreds and hundreds of years. One can go to Jerusalem and visit the Garden of Gethsemane (which means "olive press") and sit among trees that date back fifteen to sixteen hundred years. Perhaps more incredible is that the olive tree can remain productive and continue to produce fruit for the life of the tree, as long as it is cared for and pruned regularly. In this metaphor, Paul describes Israel in these same ways.

The Gentiles are described as wild olives that were grafted in. During the pruning process, smaller olive branches that are cut off are buried in a nutrient-rich soil that promotes growth. In a very short time, these branches start sending out wild olive shoots that continue to grow. These wild shoots can often be seen growing around the base of an olive tree stump that has been cut down. These young and fruitful shoots will eventually be cut and grafted into the branches of an older tree to reap from all of the benefits a mature tree has to offer. This is the picture of the Gentile church.

There are many reasons why this method of grafting is so important. First, the yield of trees and the quality of fruit that are grown from seeds or from these wild olive shoots are often very poor. To have a higher yield and better fruit, they must be grafted into something else, or another specimen must be grafted into them. The caretaker of the trees will often choose one tree for its root system and maturity and a younger tree for its leaves, flowers, or fruit. Now you have one tree that produces an abundance of high-quality fruit while benefiting from the sap of a mature root system that is often resistant to drought, diseases, and insects. The two have become one.

A second benefit of grafting is the rate of production for fruit-bearing trees. When planting a seed or a young shoot, you will wait for at least eight to ten years before full, fruit-bearing yields can be achieved. If you take these same shoots and graft them into mature trees, the growth rate drops dramatically to only two to three years before harvesting quality yields. With this understanding, many fruit producers have made a lot of money by purchasing older and unkept orchards instead of planting new ones. Through this process of pruning and grafting, broken and diseased branches can be quickly healed, and a bountiful fruit crop can be seen four times faster than by planting an entirely new orchard. Through pruning and grafting, many fruitless years of hard work and cultivating expense can be skipped.

With this basic understanding of grafting, what is Paul saying when we look past the metaphor? In Romans 11, Paul was speaking to the rapidly growing Gentile church to help her understand her place in God's plan. The Gentile church was like a wild olive branch: rapidly growing, with a great potential for producing a bountiful harvest for God. Yet the only reason they would produce such a rich, high-quality fruit was because they had been grafted into Israel. Israel provided a strong root system that could nourish them for centuries to come. Israel had been through the long and difficult years of early growth and the pruning of God and was now able to give its "disease-resistant sap" to others. The Gentile church would prosper only because of Israel.

Paul also warned against the doctrine of replacement theology that at the time was still in its infancy. The Gentiles were not to be arrogant toward the branches or Jewish people. Even though the Gentiles were already seeing more fruit than their Jewish brothers, it was only because of the wisdom that Israel had learned. For the Gentile church to cut itself off from such a root would be disastrous, as church history later proved. They were to humbly keep their eyes on God. This was God's tree, and He would graft and remove branches as He saw fit.

> For if you were cut off from what is by nature a wild olive tree, and were grafted contrary to nature into a cultivated olive tree, how much more will these who are the natural branches be grafted into their own olive tree?
>
> —ROMANS 11:24

Here again Paul warns against the arrogant idea that the Gentiles have forever replaced Israel. When the branches that were grafted in have reached their peak in fruit production, the original branches can then be added again and will enjoy the same fruitfulness. God has not forgotten or rejected Israel. They will again be restored to the same tree that God began. In the end, there will be one tree of Jews and Gentiles, all being nourished by the root of God's covenant love for Israel.

> For I do not want you, brethren, to be uninformed of this mystery—so that you will not be wise in your own estimation—*that a partial hardening has happened to Israel until the fullness of the Gentiles has come in; and so all Israel will be saved.*
>
> —ROMANS 11:25–26, EMPHASIS ADDED

Paul wanted God's plan for both the Jews and the Gentiles to be known and understood, so as to avoid pride and arrogance on the part of the Gentiles. In His amazing plan, the Gentiles would play a large part in restoring the Jews to the life-giving sap of God. This way, no one could be proud. The Jews could not claim to have blessed all of the earth without recognizing the help of the Gentiles, and the Gentiles could not claim to have blessed the earth without recognizing the wisdom and guidance of the Jewish scriptures. The only One who could receive credit would be the planter of this tree, the Lord God.

I am often asked, "How can we as Christians really support and bless Israel?" Financial gifts, prayer and intercession, and going on an Israel tour to learn are all great ways and are certainly encouraged. Yet there is one way that Christians can truly bless Israel and help fulfill the scriptures. In God's amazing plan, whether Christians are pro- or anti-Israel, all of them are helping to bless and restore Israel to her original intent. They do this by being active in local congregations and in the body of Christ.

According to Paul, Israel is not hardened forever but partially hardened for a specific amount of time. Again, Romans 11:25 says, "A partial hardening has happened to Israel *until* the fullness of the Gentiles has come in" (emphasis added). The key word in this verse is *until*. At some point in the plan of God, He will say that the fullness of the Gentiles is in. At that point, the hardness over Israel will disappear, and "all Israel will be saved" (v. 26). Every Christian church, congregation, prayer meeting, worship evening, outreach, street ministry, Bible study, and every other activity that any group of believers is involved in is helping to bring in the Gentiles. If you are active with local believers, you are contributing to the ushering in of the time when God declares that the fullness of the Gentiles has come in and the partial hardening of Israel is lifted!

It should be made clear, however, that this is not a call to prepare for "Jewish evangelism," nor is it a suggestion that we shrink back from testifying of the Lord. It is only an effort to shed light on God's overall plan. The Jewish people are destined to return to the God of Israel and His Messiah in the same way that we Christians have come to know Him: by having our hearts touched and through the conviction of sin by the Holy Spirit. The Old Testament even speaks of replacing Israel's heart of stone and making a new covenant with her. It will happen. When the partial hardening lifts from the eyes of Israel, no one will gain the honor and glory for doing so except the Lord. In that day, there will be much more talk of the Lord's enduring faithfulness, undying love, and the mercy of God than of "evangelism." The attention will be on the Lord.

God has been faithful to Israel and merciful to the rest of the earth by allowing the Christian branches to be grafted into such a rich root, full of wisdom and love. In Romans, it is clear that we need to understand the church's place in God's plan. How much more should Christians understand this today, as Israel is once again a sovereign nation after two thousand years? This is not for the Jew or the Gentile, but for the glory of God. When starting to glimpse the larger plan of God, we echo Paul's words:

> Oh, the depth of the riches both of the wisdom and knowledge of God! How unsearchable are His judgments and unfathomable His ways!
>
> —ROMANS 11:33

PART III

THE THREE ANNUAL FEASTS

Chapter 8

IMPORTANCE of FEASTS

IN RECENT YEARS, the church has begun to awaken to the value of the biblical feasts. It is becoming more common for some churches to have a basic Passover celebration in the spring or to join Messianic groups that celebrate the complete service. So much can be found of the life of the Lord Jesus in these feasts!

The question many Christians ask is, "Aren't the feasts in Leviticus a Jewish thing?" The correct answer is yes and no. Yes, the feasts are "a Jewish thing" because they were commanded to be observed by Israel throughout the generations. These feasts make up a large part of Jewish life in respect to how God relates and reveals Himself to His people. We can see this in the New Testament as well, when John refers to the feasts as the "feast of the Jews" three different times to his readers (John 5:1; 6:4; 7:2).

> The feasts are also not just "a Jewish thing" because the Lord refers to these feasts as "the feasts of the Lord" and His "appointed times." If we are truly bound to the Lord, His special times will become ours. He has revealed so much of Himself in these feasts. Jesus Himself said: If you believed Moses, you would believe Me, for He wrote about Me.
>
> —JOHN 5:46

As Christians, it would be silly for us to ignore these biblical celebrations that Moses wrote about while still praying for the God of the Bible to show Himself to us. As Christians, we are "grafted in" by faith and partake in the blessings and covenant of Israel, just as foreigners who worshiped the God of Abraham, Isaac, and Jacob were received into Israel in Old Testament times. Although Christians are not required to celebrate these feasts, a basic understanding of them would radically change most Christians' perception of the Bible. The feasts are not just "a Jewish thing"; they are a "God thing" and full of Jesus.

This chapter will be a brief overview of what the feasts were intended to be, both from a literal and a prophetic point of view. Two excellent books regarding all of the appointed times are *The Feasts of the Lord* by Kevin Howard and Marvin Rosenthal, and *God's Appointed Times* by Barney Kasdan. Rather than covering all of the feasts, we will only look at the three most important biblical festivals that required one to become a pilgrim and seek out the Lord. The three main feasts will be only mentioned here; a closer examination will be made of each one from a prophetic perspective in the next three chapters.

Leviticus 23 briefly covers all of the feasts required of Israel. It's interesting to note that regardless of the feast or when or how it was to be celebrated, they are all called the same thing: a "holy convocation." This phrase is used eleven times in Leviticus 23. The intentions of these feasts were not to be overlooked, so to understand any of them, we must first know what God meant by "holy convocation."

> Speak to the sons of Israel and say to them, "The LORD's appointed times which you shall proclaim as holy convocations."
> —LEVITICUS 23:2

The Hebrew word for convocation is *mik-rah*. *Strong's Concordance* describes this word as "something called out, i.e., a public meeting (the act, the persons, or the place); also a rehearsal." It refers to both the act of gathering of people as well as the actual event itself.

But this is not just any public meeting. When used in Scripture, this word *mik-rah* is almost always followed by the word *ko-desh*, which is translated "holy." This word *ko-desh* refers to something set apart for a special purpose. In a very literal sense, the Hebrew word for "holy convocation" means to make a public call to come to a sacred and holy rehearsal meeting. This is not like any another church get-together, but it indicates a sacred and consecrated gathering because God Himself has brought forth a call to Israel to come together, and He will be in their midst.

In Leviticus 23, there are two different Hebrew words that are translated as "feast." The first word is *mo-ahd*, which is often translated "appointed time." *Mo-ahd* means to set an appointment, as in a set time or season, for a specific assembly or festival. This particular word for "feast" refers to the weekly Sabbaths and all the Levitical holy days.

Mo-ahd also has a root meaning, "to repeat," which can mean "a signal as appointed beforehand." In other words, there are things that are to be repeated each time the preset appointed time has come. When a child has a birthday, the signals or signs that their birthday has come is to have a cake and gifts, and this is usually repeated every year. This is the same idea with the Lord's appointed times. The feasts are "signals and signs" to help us know what is on the heart of the Lord.

The second word for feast, chag, is much more specific. *Chag* is mostly used to describe the Feast of Unleavened Bread, the Feast of Weeks (Pentecost), and the Feast of Tabernacles as "pilgrimage feasts." Other festivals or appointed times could be celebrated in your home or wherever you lived. These three feasts, however, required that you make your way to the tabernacle or temple, which was first in Shiloh, then in Jerusalem. *Chag* means "feast or festival" and has its root in the word *chah-gog*, which, in the Hebrew mind-set, means "to circle, as in to circle dance or feast." By very definition, these three feasts are to be celebrated before the Lord in a joyous, party atmosphere with singing, dancing, and processions.

> Three times a year you shall celebrate a feast [*chag*] to Me. You shall observe the Feast of Unleavened Bread [the first night is Passover]; for seven days you are to eat unleavened bread, as I commanded you, at the appointed time in the month Abib, for in it you came out of Egypt. And none shall appear before Me empty-handed. Also you shall observe the Feast of the Harvest [Pentecost] of the first fruits of your labors from what you sow in the field; also the Feast of the Ingathering [Tabernacles] at the end of the year when you gather in the fruit of your labors from the field. Three times a year all your males shall appear before the Lord God.
>
> —Exodus 23:14–17

What is God's intention with these feasts of the Lord? I do not intend to go "spiritual fishing," yet when we look at these three words for feast and convocation, a remarkably familiar theme can be seen. I have shortened the Hebrew definitions presented above for the sake of clarity:

+ Convocation (*mik-rah*): public call to a holy and consecrated rehearsal meeting

+ Feast (*mo-ahd*): an appointed time that involves signals appointed beforehand
+ Feast (*chag*): specific joyful, celebratory festivals that pilgrims come to

Doesn't Hebrews 10:1 tell us that the instructions of Moses are "only a shadow of the good things to come?" More specifically, Colossians 2:16–17 tells us that even the festivals and the Sabbath are only "a mere shadow of what is to come." It appears that all of God's appointed times are really prophetic words for those who would hear them and come to Him.

I submit to you that the feasts are really a prophetic call to the Lord's salvation, promised by the prophets. By definition, the feasts of the Lord are the public calling of God for anyone to come to these holy "rehearsals" that God Himself has ordained. At these rehearsals are specific signs and signals that were appointed before the foundation of the world and represent God's desire for all mankind. These signals point to specific joyful celebrations in the presence of the Lord that all are invited to yet can only be enjoyed by those pilgrims who come. Colossians 2:16–17 bears repeating: "In respect to a festival or a new moon or a Sabbath day—things which are a mere shadow of what is to come; *but the substance belongs to Christ*" (emphasis added).

In Matthew 22, when Jesus told the parable about a king who gave a wedding feast for his son, he did not tell it by chance or accident. This idea of being invited to a feast was securely rooted in the feasts of the Lord. Furthermore, Jesus spoke this parable during the Passover season, literally days before becoming the Passover sacrifice. Since the people listening to Jesus came to Jerusalem for the Passover celebration, as required in the instructions of Moses, they understood the value and importance of coming to a feast and what would be the outcome for those who did not.

Each of these three main feasts of Passover (spring), Pentecost (early summer), and Tabernacles (fall) has a clear prophetic significance. Jesus Himself said, "Though you do not believe Me, believe the works, so that you may know and understand that the Father is in Me, and I in the Father" (John 10:38). Jesus was the perfect Passover Lamb who was sacrificed so that we can live. At the Feast of Weeks (Pentecost), the Holy Spirit was sent, meaning that the firstfruits were offered and the harvest begun. At the

Feast of Tabernacles, the end of the harvest, the Messiah returns, and God is dwelling in the midst of His people. Prophetically speaking, no one can experience the fullness of these three feasts without first becoming a pilgrim and coming up to God. We will explore each of these feasts in the Old and New Testaments in the chapters ahead.

Every major teaching of Jesus took place during a Jewish feast. If you have a basic understanding of the requirements and expectations of that particular feast, the teachings of Jesus will be revealed to you as never before. There is so much to share about each of these three feasts that I will not have room for everything in these short chapters. My hope is that what I do share will ignite something in you and that the Holy Spirit will quicken other passages to your mind. I encourage you to not ignore these revelations that the Holy Spirit will stir in you, but to follow Him to see where He is leading you.

For this reason, at the end of each chapter about the pilgrim feasts, there will be a small section entitled "For Further Study." In this section, there will be a few other recommended passages for your review and scriptural comparisons that directly relate to the context and expectations of each feast. When applying the basic understanding of each chapter, these other passages will read like fresh and new portions of Scripture. If you seek Him, you will find Him.

Chapter 9

PASSOVER

M ost Jews view Passover as many Christians view Christmas. It is an anticipated season of family gathering and for reflecting on what God has done. As you will see in the study section at the end of this chapter, many, many teachings and works of Jesus were given during the Passover season. Within the context of this feast, we can find the very essence for His coming. Throughout the Gospels, Passover was extremely important to the Lord and for Christians, and it should be for us as well.

I recently had a Spirit-filled Jewish believer tell me that at every Passover he studies a different aspect of how the Lord Jesus was the fulfillment of this feast. He has been leading Passover services for churches and congregations for almost thirty years and is still amazed at the never-ending depth of the Word of God. He said every year he learns something different about the Lord and about His Passover that he had never seen before.

The first biblical instructions with regard to the Passover are recorded in Exodus 12 and begin with the lamb. On the tenth day of the first month of the year, a lamb was to be selected, brought home, and inspected for five days to check for blemishes. The lamb had to be perfect. After the killing of the lamb on the fourteenth of the month, at twilight, the Israelites were to immediately apply the blood to the doorposts of their house. The lamb was then to be roasted over a fire and eaten that very night with unleavened bread and bitter herbs. Notice how they were to eat this feast:

> Now you shall eat it in this manner: with your loins girded, your
> sandals on your feet, and your staff in your hand; and you shall
> eat it in haste—it is the LORD's Passover.
>
> —Exodus 12:11

At the first Passover Israel was still in slavery, yet the Israelites were to be ready to leave with their families and flocks at a moment's notice. This meal was to be eaten in faith that God was about to deliver them, and they needed to be ready. Passover begins with being ready to follow God in faith.

Passover also began the Feast of Unleavened Bread. They were to eat nothing with leaven in it for seven days. This was to remind them of the haste in which they left Egypt. The Israelites were required to go through their homes and remove all of the leaven they could find. Anyone with leaven in their houses would be cut off from the people. This was not an option; this was serious business.

Throughout the years, the Passover meal has become one that is greatly revered in Jewish homes. Many traditions, which include three pieces of unleavened bread, four cups of wine, and the singing of select psalms, have been added to enhance the remembrance of the ten plagues and the exodus from Egypt. By the time of Jesus, most of these traditions were already in place. Today, a traditional Passover still includes these elements and can last up to six hours!

Since biblical times, one aspect that has always been evident during the Passover season is the search for another great deliverer, the coming of the Messiah. The Jewish nation has always known that God would someday send a Messiah to rule Israel, to be a great leader, and to point them toward God for the cleansing of all of their sins. In fact, many who understood the words of the prophets expected this Messiah to be God Himself. Since the time of Moses, Israel has often suffered both internal and external conflicts and has been in great need of God's deliverance. In the eyes of the Jewish nation, what better time for God to send this Messiah than at the Passover season?

In the time of Jesus, the Passover in Jerusalem carried many different meanings for different people. It seemed that almost everyone was looking for something. In his book *Echoes of His Presence*, Ray Vander Laan explains Passover expectations this way:

> Religious Jews were looking for forgiveness from sin. Zealots were looking for the revolutionary who would lead them to freedom. Sadducees were looking for an incident-free week so that nothing would upset their balance of power. Rome's representatives were looking for crowd control. And every Jew was looking for the Messiah. Messianic fever always gripped the thousands of pilgrims thronging the streets of Jerusalem at Passover.[1]

Imagine the Messianic fervor that surrounded Jesus as He rode into Jerusalem on what happened to be the very same day that Israelite families were choosing their Passover lamb! In the original language of the book, Matthew 21:10 says that when Jesus entered Jerusalem, the city literally was shaken by a tremor or an earthquake. This Passover would certainly be different.

For the next five days, the Pharisees and teachers of the Torah tried to find fault in Jesus but could not. Jesus was then arrested and brought before the chief priests, who could not find fault in Him, other than the prophetic truths that He spoke about Himself. After being abused by the Sanhedrin, Jesus was sent to Pilate and then to Herod, in the hope of having Him condemned to death. The Roman leader confessed several times that he could find nothing wrong with Jesus. Despite his own words of Jesus's innocence, Pilate gave in to Jewish demands and sentenced Him to death. Just like the instructions for the Passover lamb in Exodus 12, Jesus was tested for blemishes for five days and declared perfect by both Jew and Gentile. Just like the lamb, Jesus was killed as the perfect Passover sacrifice for both Jew and Gentile.

Even the exact time that Jesus died fulfilled the Passover requirements. Exodus 12:6 says that the lamb was to be killed at twilight, or "between the evenings." Ancient Jewish tradition describes this time from when the sun starts to set until it has completely gone down, or approximately 3:00 to 6:00 p.m. Mark 15:34–37 says that Jesus finally died around the ninth hour of the day. The first hour of the day was at sunrise, or approximately 6:00 a.m., which makes the ninth hour around 3:00 p.m. Jesus died at the exact time Passover lambs were being killed at twilight all over Israel, according to Moses's instructions in Exodus 12:6.

Yet before all of this took place, Jesus had what Christians call "the Last Supper." Jesus knew it as Passover.

> And He said to them, "I have earnestly desired to eat this Passover with you before I suffer."
>
> —Luke 22:15

This was not a last meal before an execution but the fulfillment of an ancient prophetic meal that would prove who He was to the world. This was the reason Jesus had come. Everything that was on the table and eaten at Passover pointed to the Lord Jesus.

During the meal Jesus said, "He who dipped his hand with Me into the bowl is the one who will betray Me" (Matt. 26:23), or, "The one for whom I shall dip the morsel and give it to him" (John 13:26). As part of the Passover meal, participants eat the bitter herbs as required in Exodus 12, which represents the bitterness of slavery. This usually is eaten by dipping some unleavened bread into a bowl of ground-up bitter herbs. This was most likely what Jesus was speaking of. With this in mind, it is interesting that it was *after* Judas ate this morsel that Satan entered him (John 13:27).

Jesus later broke the bread, saying, "Take, eat; this is my body" (Matt. 26:26). This was not ordinary bread but unleavened bread, as commanded in Exodus 12. In His teachings, Jesus compared leaven to hypocrisy, sin, and wickedness. (See Matthew 16:6; Luke 12:1.) By telling His disciples that this bread was His body, He was saying that there was no sin or hypocrisy in Him and that they could partake in His sacrifice.

Throughout a traditional Jewish dinner, there are four cups of wine, of which only three are taken for drink. The third cup is recognized and consumed toward the end of the meal and is called "the cup of redemption," to remember Israel's physical redemption from Egypt. It was most likely this cup that Jesus raised, saying, "Drink from it, all of you; for this is My blood of the covenant, which is poured out for many for the forgiveness of sins" (Matt 26:27–28).

Interestingly enough, this is not the first time that Jesus spoke of eating His flesh and drinking His blood. In John 6 Jesus made similar comments. Ironically, verse 4 tells us that He said these things during the time of the Passover.

> Truly, truly, I say to you, unless you eat the flesh of the Son of Man and drink His blood, you have no life in yourselves.
>
> —John 6:53

Toward the end of John 6, we see that many disciples turned away from the Lord and didn't follow Him any longer. For the Lord, "eating the flesh" and "drinking His blood" was at the very core of being His disciple. It still is today, but we have given it a different name: Communion. The real beginning of the church's ritual of taking Communion did not start at the Last Supper but through the Passover traditions set down over thousands of years before that. Jesus was not starting anything new but was only revealing God's true message of the Passover Seder. This is why He told His disciples that when they observed this feast and broke the unleavened bread to "do this in remembrance of [Him]" (Luke 22:19). Jesus is our Passover Lamb!

> Clean out the old leaven so that you may be a new lump, just as you are in fact unleavened. For Christ our Passover also has been sacrificed. Therefore let us celebrate the feast, not with old leaven, nor with the leaven of malice and wickedness, but with the unleavened bread of sincerity and truth.
>
> —1 CORINTHIANS 5:7–8

This next spring I encourage you to find a church or a Messianic congregation that is hosting a Passover Seder. There are many other powerful insights that you will learn at that dinner that I do not have space to get into here. As with most of these biblically mandated feasts, if you understand them, you will never see Jesus in the same way again!

FOR FURTHER STUDY IN THE CONTEXT OF PASSOVER

Read Exodus 12, the account of the first Passover.

Everything spoken in the chapters below took place during the Passover season. This was the span of eleven days from when Israel was to choose their Passover sacrifice on the tenth of the month until the end of the Feast of Unleavened Bread on the twenty-first.

+ Matthew 21–28
+ Mark 11:1–16:13
+ Luke 19:29–24:35
+ John 11:55–20:25

Read the Song of Solomon. This book is traditionally read on the Sabbath that falls during the Passover week.

In Luke 2:41–52, Jesus's family was in Jerusalem for the Passover. Notice that for three days He was "not found" by His parents. About twenty-one years later, at the same Passover time, He was "not found" for another three days.

In John 6:4–71, notice how much Jesus talks about bread. Jesus asked Philip where they were going to get bread for all of these people. The bread played an important role in the Passover celebration. Jesus also offended a lot of followers when He started talking about eating His flesh and drinking His blood (vv. 51–63). He says the exact same thing at the Last Supper.

Chapter 10

PENTECOST

IN 2007, I was invited to teach at a ministry school for training prophetic worship leaders. In the course of teaching the morning session I made a side comment about Pentecost in the Book of Leviticus, to which I received many blank and confused stares. I immediately stopped the class and asked those who knew that Pentecost was in the Old Testament to raise their hands. I was shocked that in a class of almost fifty students, no one raised their hand.

Here was a group of gifted musicians and future spiritual leaders in their early twenties, some from "cool and anointed churches," who had no understanding of the roots of the single most important event in church history. Then it hit me: perhaps the churches they represented—and the people in them—didn't have a clue either. If this describes you, the next few pages may cause you to never look at Acts 2 the same way again.

The biblical name of this feast is the Feast of Weeks, or *Shah-vu-ot*. This feast started fifty days, or seven complete Sabbaths, after Passover, which is where we get the Greek name "Pentecost," as it means "fiftieth." For the sake of clarity, I will continue to refer to the feast as *Shah-vu-ot*, since that is what our first-century brethren called it, and it will better connect Acts 2 with the Old Testament. I encourage you to read Leviticus 23:15–22, as it records Moses's instructions for this feast that include a few curious details that we will look at in a moment.

Quite simply, Shah-vu-ot is the beginning of the summer wheat harvest. On the fiftieth day after Passover, the Israelites were to present the first-fruits of their grain as an offering to the Lord. Yet before you could give your offering to the Lord, you must first have harvested your fields. In Leviticus 23:22 Moses gives specific instructions on how to do this:

> When you reap the harvest of your land, moreover, you shall not reap to the very corners of your field nor gather the gleaning of

your harvest; you are to leave them for the needy and the alien. I am the LORD your God.

—LEVITICUS 23:22

No one was to go without. Even the poor or the alien could follow the harvesters and gather what they needed and offer something to the Lord. Then, after the fields were harvested, they were to bring the firstfruits of their grain to the Lord. This was a joyous celebration that focused on the Lord's lifegiving provision and remembered His deliverance. Everyone in Israel was to rejoice before the Lord, whether they owned fields or were servants, strangers, widows, or orphans. No one was to be left out.

A tradition in Israel soon arose where specific Bible passages were read during this time. Those passages read were Ezekiel 1:1–28; 3:12; Habakkuk 2:20; 3:19; and the entire Book of Ruth. At some point during the first century, the rabbis realized that the giving of the Torah to Moses on Sinai happened in the same month, and possibly on the same day, as the first day of *Shah-vu-ot*. Because of this, Exodus 19–20 were added to the readings, and the giving of the Torah was also commemorated.

The choosing of these scriptures by the rabbis to be read during this feast did not occur as a random coincidence. Before moving any further, it is imperative that we know which scriptures were being publicly read during *Shah-vu-ot*, long before Acts 2. I encourage you to read them in their entirety for deeper study, but here are just a few of the verses. Perhaps they might remind you of something.

> As I looked, behold, *a storm wind* was coming from the north, a great cloud *with fire flashing forth continually* and a bright light around it, and in its midst something like glowing metal in the midst of the fire.
>
> —EZEKIEL 1:4, EMPHASIS ADDED

> But *the* LORD *is in His holy temple.* Let all the earth be silent before Him.
>
> —HABAKKUK 2:20, EMPHASIS ADDED

> And Ruth the Moabitess said to Naomi, "Please let me go to the field and glean among the ears of grain after one in whose sight

I may find favor." And she said to her, "Go, my daughter." So she departed and went and gleaned in the field after the reapers.

—RUTH 2:2–3

Remember Moses's instructions in Leviticus 23:22 about how to harvest your field? It is because Boaz obeyed the instructions of Moses and did not glean his fields entirely that he met Ruth. The context for the entire Book of Ruth is rooted in the Old Testament Feast of Pentecost.

Now Mount Sinai was all in smoke because the LORD *descended upon it in fire*; and its smoke ascended like the smoke of a furnace, and *the whole mountain quaked violently*.

—EXODUS 19:18, EMPHASIS ADDED

Can you imagine going into the temple for the first day of *Shah-vu-ot* during one particularly turbulent year around A.D. 33? After hearing these passages read again like the year before, you leave the temple prayers around the third hour of the day (9:00 a.m.) and encounter this:

When the day of Pentecost [*Shah-vu-ot*] had come, they were all together in one place. And suddenly there *came from heaven a noise like a violent rushing wind*, and it filled the whole house where they were sitting. And there appeared to them *tongues as of fire distributing themselves*, and they rested on each one of them. And they were all filled with the Holy Spirit and began to speak with other tongues, as the Spirit was giving them utterance. Now there were Jews living in Jerusalem, devout men from every nation under heaven. And *when this sound occurred*, the crowd came together, and were bewildered because each one of them was hearing them speak in his own language.

—ACTS 2:1–6, EMPHASIS ADDED

At the temple, you had just listened to the description of Ezekiel's encounter with God—a strong wind and a flashing fire dancing about. You may have possibly heard Moses's description of the giving of God's instructions on Sinai—thunder and lightning flashes, the Lord descending in fire, and the violent shaking of the mountain. As you leave the temple, you suddenly hear this noisy, violent, storm-like wind that draws you to a place that is being shaken and where fire is coming down on men as they proclaim the mighty deeds of God! In this context of Old Testament *Shah-vu-ot*, it is easy to see why men from all over the first-century world were in Jerusalem for this pilgrimage feast. It is also why Peter instantly had a crowd of thousands standing in amazement and open to whatever God was doing.

We wrongly assume that Pentecost, or *Shah-vu-ot*, started and ended in Acts 2. The prophetic symbolism of *Shah-vu-ot* can be seen to have expressed itself throughout the entire week, from chapters 2–5. The initial fulfillments were great, but there were many other things that confirmed to these Jewish apostles that this really was the true fulfillment of *Shah-vu-ot*. The firstfruits were being given to God, needs were being met, and the harvest was beginning to be brought in. There was great rejoicing! This truly was Pentecost!

> So then, those who had received his word were baptized; and
> that day there were added about *three thousand souls*.
> —ACTS 2:41, EMPHASIS ADDED

Why is the number three thousand significant? During the first century, *Shah-vu-ot* began to also commemorate the giving of God's instructions at Mount Sinai. It was at this time, three thousand Israelites were killed for their rebellion and unbelief (Exod. 32:28). At the sending of the Holy Spirit, three thousand Israelites were saved through belief in Jesus. Furthermore, these two events may have possibly occurred on the exact same day. The first fruit of the Torah was death. The first fruit of the Spirit is life!

> For *there was not a needy person among them*, for all who were
> owners of land or houses would sell them and bring the proceeds
> of the sales and lay them at the apostles' feet, and they would be
> distributed to each as any had need.
> —ACTS 4:34–35, EMPHASIS ADDED

At *Shah-vu-ot*, everyone's needs were to be met, and no one was to be left out. Remember the story of Ruth? As a result of *Shah-vu-ot*, a man born in Bethlehem, Boaz, married Ruth (a Gentile) and welcomed her into Israel. It is also because of *Shah-vu-ot* that another man born in Bethlehem, Jesus, married us (Gentiles) and welcomed us into Israel.

As for the harvest, it kept coming and coming and coming:

And the Lord was adding to their number day by day those who were being saved.

—Acts 2:47

But many of those who had heard the message believed; and the number of the men came to be about five thousand.

—Acts 4:4

And all the more believers in the Lord, multitudes of men and women, were constantly added to their number.

—Acts 5:14

The word of God kept on spreading; and the number of the disciples continued to increase greatly in Jerusalem, and a great many of the priests were becoming obedient to the faith.

—Acts 6:7

The incredible numbers that came to faith during the time of this feast was only the first fruit of the harvest. The next feast on the calendar is the Feast of the Ingathering, or the Feast of Tabernacles. Living in the last days, we need to realize that the next prophetic feast is upon us. Jesus said that the full harvest was to occur at the end of the age!

For Further Study in the Context of the Feast of Weeks

+ Read Ezekiel 1:1–28; 3:12; Habakkuk 2:20–3:19; and Exodus 19–20.
+ Read the events of the entire week of the feast of Pentecost in Acts 2–5.
+ Read the Book of Ruth.
+ Compare the events surrounding the giving of the Torah and the sending of the Holy Spirit.

Chapter 11

FEAST of TABERNACLES

A S WITH MOST of these feasts, the majority of Christians know only the basic prophetic fulfillment of these biblical celebrations. As commonly viewed through the eyes of the church, the Feast of Tabernacles (*Sukkot* in Hebrew) represents a time when Jesus returns and establishes His rule on the earth. Although this is true, there is so much more that will enhance our understanding of this feast, both of the past and the future. Understanding the history behind any account adds much depth and meaning to the known results. This is why a strong love for the Old Testament is paramount to our relationship with the Lord Jesus.

> On exactly the fifteenth day of the seventh month, when you have gathered in the crops of the land, you shall celebrate the feast of the LORD for seven days, with a rest on the first day and a rest on the eighth day. Now on the first day you shall take for yourselves the foliage of beautiful trees, palm branches and boughs of leafy trees and willows of the brook, and you shall rejoice before the LORD your God for seven days.
>
> —LEVITICUS 23:39–40

The Old Testament instructions for the Feast of the Ingathering (or Feast of the Tabernacles) were pretty simple. After you bring in your harvest, come to Jerusalem, build a booth out of branches to live in for seven days, and celebrate before the Lord. It was a time to remember God's kindnesses and mercies toward Israel in the past, as well as His goodness and provision at the present time in allowing Israel to bring in the harvest. All of Israel came together to rejoice and dance before the Lord. It was one of the most joyous and festive of all of the feasts.

In the midst of the celebration, there was a clear demonstration of the people's sense of awe of God and of His power. Israel was to live in these booths or tabernacles in order to remember the time of their living in tents in the desert, grouped around the tabernacle of God. Not only did God provide for Israel in the desert, but He was also in their midst. In his book *The Temple: Its Ministry and Services*, Alfred Edersheim states, "According to Jewish tradition, the pillar of cloud by day and of fire by night had first appeared to Israel on the fifteenth of Tishri, the first day of the feast."[1] It is also said to be the same day that Moses came down from Sinai with instructions to build the tabernacle. A thousand years later, it was the same day that Solomon dedicated the temple, as fire came down from heaven and God's glory filled the temple. After the time of David, a traditional reading for the beginning and end of the feast was taken from Psalm 29, with its mention of the powerful voice of the Lord. This entire feast was about the almighty God living in their midst within the context of obvious supernatural evidence.

Although the Bible doesn't mention it, many Bible scholars believe it is very likely that Jesus was born around the time of this feast. It is entirely plausible that the Romans chose to take their census around the time of a local traditional celebration, such as this feast. That would also explain why there was "no room at the inn," due to the pilgrimage, and why Jewish shepherds were so affected by the glorious angelic visitations. While angelic visitations will always get your attention, it may have especially affected the shepherds, knowing that the Feast of Tabernacles was a time when God had visibly shown His presence through supernatural means in Israel's history. Isaiah 7:14 says, "A virgin will be with child and bear a son, and she will call His name Immanuel." This name, Immanuel, means "God with us," and John 1:14 tells us, "The Word became flesh, and dwelt among us, and we saw His glory." This particular feast was meant to joyously commemorate when the Almighty lived in their midst in the desert. What a perfect time for the birth of the Savior of the world, who was called to the lost sheep of Israel!

By the first century, a daily festive tradition called the water libation was being observed. At sunrise, a priest would take a golden pitcher to the pool of Siloam and bring a liter of water back to the temple through the Water Gate. This priest would be followed by a dancing and rejoicing crowd that praised the Lord for the year's harvest and prayed for rain for the next season. The crowd would wave palm branches and shout "Hosanna!" while singing Psalm 118:25: "Save now, I pray, O LORD; O LORD, I pray, send now prosperity."

As the priest reached the altar and began pouring out the water around it, the celebration intensified. The Levites would begin to sing Isaiah 12:3: "Therefore you will joyously draw water from the springs of salvation." Each day this tradition would build in excitement and praise, until the last day when the priest would walk around the altar seven times before pouring out the water. This was such an exciting event that some ancient rabbis have stated that you have never experienced real joy unless you have been at the temple on the last day of the feast.[2]

It is a common Christian misunderstanding that ancient or present-day Jews who do not accept Jesus as the Messiah do not understand the prophetic symbolism in Israel's history. This is simply not accurate. This particular tradition of pouring out water was widely viewed with clear Messianic connotations. To again take from Alfred Edersheim's book *The Temple*, he writes, "The main and real application [of this ritual] was to the future outpouring of the Holy Spirit,"[3] as predicted by the prophet Isaiah. As the water was poured out and the Levites sang Isaiah 12:3, the festival crowds viewed this as a prophetic act. This pouring out of water represented to them a day when the water of God's Spirit would be poured out on Israel. Their prayers would turn to intercession as they looked to the promises of prophets like Zechariah, who prophesied that the Messiah would come and reign in Jerusalem. The Messiah will come! What better time than at this feast?

It is in this context of celebration and Messianic expectation that Jesus shouted above the crowd and stopped this feast in its tracks:

> Now on the last day, the great day of the feast, Jesus stood and cried out, saying, "If anyone is thirsty, let him come to Me and drink. He who believes in Me, as the Scripture said, 'From his innermost being will flow rivers of living water.'" But this He spoke of the Spirit, whom those who believed in Him were to receive; for the Spirit was not yet given, because Jesus was not yet glorified. Some of the people therefore, when they heard these words, were saying, "This certainly is the Prophet." Others were saying, "This is the Christ." Still others were saying, "Surely the Christ is not going to come from Galilee, is He?"
>
> —JOHN 7:37–41

John understood the Jewish symbolism of the priest's water that represented the Spirit of God poured out on Israel. Because of this, he clearly made this connection for his readers in verse 39. The crowd that was there also understood this parallel that Jesus was making, since everyone started saying, "This certainly is the Prophet" and "This is the Christ." This water did represent the Spirit, and by faith in Jesus, it would flow from within!

One of the clearest passages about the Messiah in the midst of the Feast of Tabernacles is written in Zechariah:

> Then it will come about that any who are left of all the nations that went against Jerusalem *will go up from year to year to worship the King, the* Lord *of hosts, and to celebrate the Feast of Booths.* And it will be that whichever of the families of the earth does not go up to Jerusalem to worship the King, the Lord of hosts, there will be no rain on them. If the family of Egypt does not go up or enter, then no rain will fall on them; it will be the plague with which the Lord smites the nations who do not go up to celebrate the Feast of Booths. This will be the punishment of Egypt, and the punishment of all the nations who do not go up to celebrate the Feast of Booths.
>
> —Zechariah 14:16–19, emphasis added

Notice that during the time of the Messiah's reign in Jerusalem, this feast is not a "Jewish thing" but is required of all the nations. This is not about worshiping in a Jewish way but about the nations recognizing that the King, the Lord of hosts, is God dwelling among His people. This is the literal fulfillment of the Feast of Tabernacles, and the nations that do not come to acknowledge this will be seen as rejecting the authority of God Himself.

It is not a coincidence that the punishment for these nations is no rain. Part of the Feast of the Tabernacle's celebration, and the tradition of pouring water around the altar, was to pray for rain for the coming year. Water and rain were seen as being symbolic of God's Spirit. How can you have God's Spirit (rain) poured out on your nation if you do not come to recognize that God, the Lord of hosts, reigns in Jerusalem? Whether this refers to literal or spiritual rain, it is sobering to imagine the potential impact that an entire nation would feel with no rain and no mercy or protection from God for one full year.

As stated many times in this book, God's desire throughout the Bible is to live among His people. You can see this in the Genesis story of Eden, in the instructions of Moses, in the Prophets, and throughout the New Testament. By the end of time, it will have happened. For believers in the Lord Jesus, we can constantly live as if we were celebrating this feast right now, since this Living Water is now in us! God is dwelling in us, and we have seen His glory! How much more will this be true when we hear "a loud voice from the throne, saying, 'Behold, the tabernacle of God is among men, and He will dwell among them, and they shall be His people, and God Himself will be among them'" (Rev. 21:3)!

FOR FURTHER STUDY IN THE CONTEXT OF THE FEAST OF TABERNACLES

+ Read Zechariah 12–14 and compare it with Revelation 19–21.

+ Reread the Christmas story of Luke 2.

+ Read John 7–9 in the context of this feast, and notice the number of times that Jesus spoke of Himself as God or equal to God in these chapters.

+ Compare the expectations of this feast to the account of when Jesus was transfigured (Matt. 17:1–9; Mark 9:2–8; Luke 9:28–36), and notice Peter's comments.

PART IV

PRESENT-DAY THEMES

Chapter 12

THE VALUE of JERUSALEM

T HERE IS NO city on Earth that can compare in value to that of Jerusalem. Most Christians revere Jerusalem as the city where Jesus walked, was crucified, and rose from the dead. However, as we can see from the scriptures, it was valuable to the Lord long before the time of Jesus. With over eight hundred references to Jerusalem in the Bible, there is much that can be learned about it. But there is only one possible reason that this city has seen such spiritual and physical conflict since the beginning of time, and that is because God Himself has chosen this earthly city to dwell in and to establish His name among men.

There was always something different about the land that God promised to Abraham. It was the place that God desired for man to come to form a relationship with Him. In Genesis 17:8, God gives to Abraham's descendants "all the land of Canaan, for an everlasting possession; and I will be their God." Even the name of Canaan was prophetic of God's desire for a relationship with man. In Hebrew, *Canaan* is taken from the word *kah-nah*, which means "to bend the knee or to humble oneself." God's plan for the descendants of Abraham was that they would live in the land of humility on bended knees. It was in this land that He would be their God. Years after this promise, God spoke to Abraham to take Isaac to a particular place within Canaan:

> He said, "Take now your son, your only son, whom you love, Isaac, and *go to the land of Moriah,* and offer him there as a burnt offering on one of the mountains of which I will tell you."
> —GENESIS 22:2, EMPHASIS ADDED

Here again names are significant. In Hebrew *Moriah* (*Moh-ri-yah*) means "seen of Yahweh." Quite literally, God was saying to Abraham, "Go to the land that I am looking at, and there I will show you a specific mountain." We all know what happened when they got there.

After Isaac was replaced by the sacrificial ram, Abraham declared, "In the mount of the LORD it will be provided" (Gen. 22:14). In the eyes of Abraham, the mountain of the Lord was a literal and holy place, not just a figure of speech. It was where God stepped in and provided a sacrifice to save Abraham's descendants. This happened on a specific mountain, Mount Moriah, the mountain that is "seen by Yahweh." Anytime in Scripture when the prophets speak of "the mountain of the Lord," it is specifically referring to this mountain and this event.

Over four hundred years later, all of Israel knew of and dreamed of this land promised to their forefather Abraham. Now that God had delivered Israel from Egypt, they were on their way to live in this land of promise. Soon Moses began speaking to God about this specific and unique location that He had promised to bring them to:

> You will bring them and plant them in the mountain of Your inheritance, the place, O LORD, which You have made for Your dwelling, the sanctuary, O LORD, which Your hands have established.
>
> —EXODUS 15:17

This was their first clue. God was bringing them to the mountain of His inheritance and the place where He dwells. But the clues would not stop there. Throughout the time in the desert, Moses kept speaking of this unique location, what it would be like, and what God wanted them to do there. It became known simply as "the place." This is what Moses said Israel should expect at "the place that He chooses":

+ **The Lord dwells there:** Exod. 15:17; Deut. 12:5; 12:11

+ **His name would be established:** Deut. 12:5; 12:21; 14:23–24; 16:6

+ **God has chosen this place:** Deut. 12:18; 12:26; 14:25; 16:7; 18:6

+ **God promised it, prepared it, and would give it to them:** Exod. 23:20; Num. 10:29; 14:40

+ **Worship, sacrifices, and offerings:** Deut. 12:6; 12:11; 12:13–14; 26:2

+ **Eating before the Lord:** Deut. 12:7; 12:18; 14:23

- **Rejoicing before the Lord:** Deut. 12:7; 12:18; 16:11
- **Celebrating the feasts:** Deut. 15:20; 16:15–16
- **Sacrificing of the Passover lamb:** Deut. 16:2; 16:6–7
- **Works of your hand are blessed:** Deut. 12:7; 16:15
- **Disputes are settled:** Deut. 17:8
- **Judgments and verdicts are declared:** Deut. 17:10
- **Levites come to serve the Lord:** Deut. 18:7
- **Reading of the instructions of Moses to all of Israel:** Deut. 31:11

Who wouldn't want to live in a place like this? God would be in the midst of His people and in their everyday affairs. After slavery in Egypt, this description probably sounded like…well…*heaven.* But first, they must enter and start to take this Promised Land.

Four hundred years after the time Moses, in the time of David, Israel still viewed their many battles as fulfilling what Moses and Joshua had told them to do. David had conquered Jerusalem, had established it as the seat of power in Israel, and was becoming widely loved as king. Yet with the many years and struggles since their deliverance from slavery, they still had not found this "place" that Moses spoke of—or maybe they had.

This revelation hit David quite unexpectedly. In 1 Chronicles 21, David had sinned by numbering the people, and a devastating plague was released on Israel. At the word of the Lord, David went to Ornan's threshing floor to build an altar and to call on the Lord.

> Then David built an altar to the LORD there and offered burnt offerings and peace offerings. And he called to the LORD and He *answered him with fire from heaven on the altar of burnt offering.*
> —1 CHRONICLES 21:26, EMPHASIS ADDED

This must have been a shock for David. God had descended in fire on Sinai, and fire had come forth out of the tabernacle in the desert, but no one had ever seen fire come down from heaven. This place was unique, as if God Himself dwelled here. David realized that this was *the* place, the house of the Lord God (1 Chron. 22:1). Israel could rest because they were finally at the place the Lord had chosen for them. Years after David's death, as Solomon began building the temple, the Bible tied the loose ends of God's intentions together.

> Then Solomon began to build *the house of the* LORD *in Jerusalem on Mount Moriah*, where the Lord had appeared to his father David, at the place that David had prepared on the threshing floor of Ornan the Jebusite.
>
> —2 CHRONICLES 3:1, EMPHASIS ADDED

The same mountain where God led Abraham was the same mountain where God led David and was the same mountain where God would lead all of Israel at the temple. This literally was Mount Moriah, the mountain of the Lord, the mountain that is "seen by Yahweh."

After the temple was completed and dedicated by Solomon, the Lord visited Solomon in response to his prayers:

> Then the LORD appeared to Solomon at night and said to him, "I have heard your prayer and have *chosen this place for Myself* as a house of sacrifice....Now My eyes will be open and My ears attentive to the prayer offered in this place. For now I have chosen and consecrated this house that My name may be there forever, and *My eyes and My heart will be there perpetually.*"
>
> —2 CHRONICLES 7:12, 15–16, EMPHASIS ADDED

I suggest to you that the Lord's words here had nothing to do with the temple itself. God had already chosen this place for sacrifice, as demonstrated through Isaac and David. His eyes and ears were attentive to the prayers offered there because this was the mount "seen by Yahweh." He had already chosen this place, and His name would be there forever, just as He had told Moses four hundred years before. I believe there is no new revelation spoken here, but rather a reminder of God's faithfulness over a period of hundreds of years. In no way does this diminish the importance of the temple, but rather it lovingly tells Israel that Jerusalem is exactly where God wants them to be. What could be better than that?

Later, in the time of the prophets, Jerusalem started to take on an expanded identity. The prophets began speaking of the city as a place for all nations to seek the Lord. Jeremiah said there will be a time when "they will call Jerusalem 'The Throne of the LORD,' and all the nations will be gathered to it, to Jerusalem" (Jer. 3:17). Micah said, "Many nations will come and say, 'Come and let us go up to the mountain of the LORD…for from Zion will go forth the law [literally teaching or instruction], even the word of the LORD from Jerusalem'" (Mic. 4:2). Zechariah even speaks of punishment for the nations that do not go up to Jerusalem to worship the King (Zech. 14:17). The prophets spoke of Jerusalem not just as the Jewish capital but as the central focus for the worship of God of all the earth.

By the time of Jesus, the centrality of Jerusalem in God's plan had not decayed. Some of Jesus's best teachings and works were in Jerusalem during the pilgrimage feasts. As the time came for His own sacrifice on Mount Moriah, Luke 9:51 says that Jesus "was determined to go to Jerusalem." Matthew 16:21 says, "Jesus began to show His disciples that He must go to Jerusalem." What was the big deal? Again, we look to the instructions of Moses. In Deuteronomy 16, Moses said that this place—Jerusalem—was where God wanted Israel to sacrifice the Passover lamb. If Jesus really was the Passover Lamb, He could only die in one city—Jerusalem—in accordance with God's instructions.

Jesus taught and ministered in Jerusalem. By His death and resurrection He fulfilled the Torah in Jerusalem. According to the prophets, He will return and rule from Jerusalem. Nations will worship Him in Jerusalem. In that day disputes will be settled, and judgments and verdicts will be declared by Him in Jerusalem, just as Moses said would happen at that place. There is no other place on the earth that has such a destiny.

Today many Christians make the mistake of viewing a lot of these prophetic passages about Israel and Jerusalem as vague and general. For Abraham, Moses, David, and even the Lord Himself, these words were about a very real and literal place. If we begin to look at them the same way, we will understand that God is much more tangible and interested in us and in our world than we first realized. This is why almost every Christian who goes to Jerusalem for the first time is so strongly affected. Surely this is "the place"!

> For the LORD has chosen Zion; He has desired it for His habitation. This is My resting place forever; here I will dwell, for I have desired it.
>
> —PSALM 132:13–14

Chapter 13

"MAKING *ALIYAH*"

So much has happened since Israel declared her independence on May 14, 1948, that has caused the Jewish and Christian worlds to stop and take notice. But none is more obvious and significant than Jews from all over the world fulfilling ancient prophecy by returning to the land promised to Abraham. In the eyes of recorded history, this is simply amazing. No other people group on Earth has ever been conquered and dispersed to the nations twice, only to return two times to the exact same piece of real estate as an identifiable people and a sovereign nation thousands of years later.

God's promise to regather Israel is one of the most repeated in all of Scripture. According to the Jewish prophets, this gathering of Israel to her ancient land will usher in the greatest spiritual revival in Israel's history. It is happening in our time, and we would be foolish not to recognize its importance. God is calling His people back to His land and back to Himself.

The Israeli government describes Jews returning to Israel from the nations as "making *aliyah*." In Hebrew, *aliyah* means "to go up" and actually refers to an upper room of a house. Sound familiar? Ironically, the first time the root of this word is used in Scripture is in Exodus when it describes Moses "going up" to meet with God:

> The LORD came down on Mount Sinai, to the top of the mountain; and the LORD called Moses to the top of the mountain, and Moses went up.
>
> —EXODUS 19:20

Moses went up to meet with God on Sinai where he received the Ten Commandments. The intention of *aliyah* (going up) is not just to go somewhere but to go up and meet with God. The Lord is bringing the Jewish people back to the land He promised to Abraham, not only to keep His promise but also to dwell among them as their God. His plan was always to live among His people, and He is bringing that plan to pass.

Why should it matter to Christians if Jews are returning to Israel? For those of us who love the Lord and His Word, we are watching ancient biblical prophecy be fulfilled before our eyes. News headlines are confirming the accuracy of the prophets, proving the scriptures are true, and demonstrating the faithfulness of the God of Israel. Furthermore, this unfolding of biblical prophecy points to what both Jews and Christians have prayed for: the coming of the Messiah. The more we read the scriptures, the more their accuracy is seen.

> Then it will happen on that day that the LORD will again recover *the second time* with His hand the remnant of His people, who will remain, from Assyria, Egypt, Pathros, Cush, Elam, Shinar, Hamath, and from the islands of the sea. And He will lift up a standard for the nations and assemble the banished ones of Israel, and will gather the dispersed of Judah from the four corners of the earth.
>
> —ISAIAH 11:11–12, EMPHASIS ADDED

Isaiah states that the Lord will recover His people "the second time." In history, Jews were regathered the first time during the time of Ezra and Nehemiah. This was after they were held as captives for seventy years in Babylon and Assyria. Jews would remain in the land until after the time of Jesus, when the Romans destroyed the temple and threw the Jews from the land for the second time. Soon after 135 A.D., the Romans then renamed the land "Syria Palaestina" ("Palestine" in English) after Israel's archenemies, the Philistines, in the hope of removing all Jewish identity from the land promised to Abraham, Isaac, and Jacob. It was not until eighteen hundred years later that modern Zionism planted the seed of desire for many Jews to return to this forsaken land "the second time."

God seemingly placed His own approval on this movement the same week that Israel became a sovereign nation on May 14, 1948. Every week in synagogues all over the world, observant Jews read preset passages of Scripture called the Torah portion and the Haftorah portion. The Torah portion is read from the Torah, or the first five books of Moses, and the Haftorah portion comes from the writings and the prophets. It just so happened that the very week Israel became a nation for the first time in over two thousand years, observant Jews all over the world heard these verses read from Amos in the Haftorah portion:

> Also I will restore the captivity of My people Israel, and they will rebuild the ruined cities and live in them....I *will also plant them on their land, and they will not again be rooted out from their land* which I have given them.

—AMOS 9:14–15, EMPHASIS ADDED

How could you not be touched when the Almighty confirms His faithfulness to His people? Many Jewish accounts of that week and the weeks that followed recall the feeling of writing another book of Scripture—or perhaps just fulfilling one. It was a time when many Jews felt joined to their ancient ancestors who left Egypt for the Promised Land. Jeremiah the prophet alluded to this comparison thousands of years before 1948:

> "Therefore behold, days are coming," declares the LORD, "when it will no longer be said, 'As the LORD lives, who brought up the sons of Israel out of the land of Egypt,' but, 'As the LORD lives, who brought up the sons of Israel from the land of the north and from all the countries where He had banished them.' For I will restore them to their own land which I gave to their fathers."

—JEREMIAH 16:14–15

Jeremiah said that the exodus from the four corners of the earth would be greater and more miraculous then the exodus from Egypt. Today, as you read these words, Jeremiah's words are already true. Most Bible scholars say that one to two million people left Egypt. As of the end of 2007, there are an estimated 5.5 million Jews who now live in Israel. Although the percentages of Jews returning to Israel dropped slightly in 2007, according to the Jewish People Policy Planning Institute, the Jewish population will continue to grow to more than 6.2 million by 2020.[1] This is God's doing; He is bringing them together for a purpose.

> For I will take you from the nations, gather you from all the lands and bring you into your own land. Then I will sprinkle clean water on you, and you will be clean; I will cleanse you from all your filthiness and from all your idols. Moreover, I will give you a new heart and put a new spirit within you; and I will remove the

heart of stone from your flesh and give you a heart of flesh. I will put My Spirit within you and cause you to walk in My statutes, and you will be careful to observe My ordinances. You will live in the land that I gave to your forefathers; so you will be My people, and I will be your God.

—EZEKIEL 36:24–28

The intention of the Lord is to bring the Jewish nation together and cleanse the people from their sins. The popular "Christianized" verse about removing a stony heart and replacing it with a heart of flesh and placing His spirit in us is in similar context to what He plans to do with Israel when He brings them back to their land! Throughout the scriptures and even in the Torah, God repeatedly states His desire for Israel to be His people and for Him to be their God. He is about to bring this to pass in our day.

> Thus says the LORD, "I will return to Zion and *will dwell in the midst of Jerusalem.*" ... Thus says the LORD of hosts, "Behold, I am going to save My people from the land of the east and from the land of the west; and *I will bring them back and they will live in the midst of Jerusalem*; and they shall be My people, and I will be their God in truth and righteousness."
>
> —ZECHARIAH 8:3, 7–8, EMPHASIS ADDED

The return of the Jewish Messiah is directly linked to the regathering of Israel. He is bringing the Jewish people back from the ends of the earth to be ready to live with Him in Jerusalem. From the very beginning, the Lord has always desired to dwell among men. He is working all of human history to this end: to be God to His beloved creation. He will prepare their hearts and pour out His Spirit on Israel.

> I will pour out on the house of David and on the inhabitants of Jerusalem, the Spirit of grace and of supplication, so that they will look on Me whom they have pierced; and they will mourn for Him, as one mourns for an only son, and they will weep bitterly over Him like the bitter weeping over a firstborn.
>
> —ZECHARIAH 12:10

It will happen; in fact, many in Jerusalem with tell you that the trickle of this promised outpouring has already begun. There are true stories all over

Israel of rabbis, politicians, military generals, and many others who have begun crying out to Jesus, the Jewish Messiah. This was not done by missionaries but by the word of the prophets and the hand of their God. The Lord will bring His nation full circle, and as Romans 11:26 proclaims, "so all Israel will be saved."

We have briefly covered just a few of the scriptures pertaining to God's plan for the Jewish nation to make *aliyah*. God is not silent regarding His desires for Jews to return to the land of Israel, as the vast amount of scriptures proves. Even recently there have been reports about more and more Jewish actors and comedians in the West saying they have this "growing inward desire" to visit or even move to Israel. God is still calling His people to "come up."

From Genesis to Revelation, God has always desired to dwell in the midst of His people. We as Christians at the end of this age have the opportunity to not only watch it happen, but also to partake and to be joined in the fulfillment of the everlasting faithfulness of God. Both Old and New Testament prophets agree: when Israel is regathered to her land, the outpouring of the Holy Spirit on Israel and the return of Jesus, the Jewish Messiah, are not far behind. Come quickly, Lord Jesus!

Chapter 14

ISRAEL TODAY

REGARDLESS OF YOUR theology, political leaning, or personal opinion about the present-day nation of Israel, it is hard to ignore that something unique is happening in that nation. The nation and its people are peppered with supernatural encounters and groundbreaking discoveries. We could call them coincidence or luck...or we could just agree with the truth of the Bible. The truth is that God has not forsaken or rejected the Jewish people but has continued to demonstrate His faithfulness to them, as the nations of the earth look on.

One of these obvious examples of miraculous occurrences has to do with the land itself. In 1867, when Mark Twain visited what was then called Palestine, he wrote: "Palestine sits in sackcloth and ashes. Over it broods the spell of a curse that has withered its field and fettered its energies....A desolate country whose soil is rich enough, but is given over wholly to weeds...a silent, mournful expanse...a desolation."[1] One hundred fifty years later, deserts have been turned into vast forests, and the nation of Israel has become one of the largest exporters of flowers, fruits, and vegetables in the Middle East and Europe.

This responsiveness of the land was prophesied by Ezekiel. We often think of prophetic words being spoken to people, but here it is spoken directly to aspects of the land of Israel itself:

> Therefore prophesy concerning the land of Israel and *say to the mountains and to the hills, to the ravines and to the valleys,* "Thus says the Lord God, 'Behold, I have spoken in My jealousy and in My wrath because you have endured the insults of the nations.' Therefore thus says the Lord God, 'I have sworn that surely the nations which are around you will themselves endure their insults. *But you, O mountains of Israel, you will put forth your branches and bear your fruit for My people Israel; for they will soon come.* For, behold, I am for you, and I will turn to you, and you will be cultivated and sown. I will multiply men on you, all the house of Israel, all of it; and the cities will be inhabited and

the waste places will be rebuilt. I will multiply on you man and beast; and they will increase and be fruitful; and I will cause you to be inhabited as you were formerly and will treat you better than at the first. Thus you will know that I am the Lord. Yes, I will cause men—My people Israel—to walk on you and possess you, so that you will become their inheritance and never again bereave them of children.

—EZEKIEL 36:6–12

The prophecy states that the land itself will respond to Jewish ownership by putting forth branches and bearing fruit. The land is promised that Israel's cities will be rebuilt and that both man and beast will increase and be fruitful. It is happening today. In the months following the 2005 Israeli withdrawal from Gaza, there were reports that the new Palestinian owners of vast vegetable greenhouses were requesting help from the previous Israeli owners. For some reason they were having trouble producing half of the previous amount of produce as the Israeli owners. I believe this does not speak of any "Arab curse" but of the unique Jewish union with the land as prophesied in Ezekiel 36.

Another undeniable example of God's hand on the nation of Israel can be plainly seen in their military history. Many of Israel's wars since 1948 read like Old Testament battle stories. In Israel's War of Independence, Israel was being invaded by twelve well-equipped and well-armed Arab armies. The day the war started, Israel had no planes, one tank, three armored vehicles, and five cannons, which were still en route from Europe—not to mention being surrounded by seven Arab nations intent on Israel's destruction. What should have been a swift destruction of the young Jewish state, taking a few days at the most, brought a truce over a year later, to the embarrassment of the Arab nations. There are many stories of angelic appearances defending Israeli fighters and of an indescribable fear coming over the invading Arab armies.[2]

In the Six Day War in 1967, several Arab nations tried again. By itself, the Israeli Air Force destroyed over four hundred enemy planes in one day and had complete air superiority in three hours. Surrendered Egyptian tank brigades reported fighting against numbers of Israeli tanks that more than doubled and tripled their actual numbers. By the end of these six days, Israel had taken three and a half times more land than they started with.

It is reported that each time Israel has been invaded, top generals in the Pentagon and the Kremlin have said destruction of Israel was inevitable. Yet not only does Israel survive, but she also goes on to prosper, as God has set a table for Israel in the presence of her enemies (Ps. 23:5). With outcomes like this, it is no wonder that the United States Military Academy at West Point reportedly does not study the wars of Israel due to their apparently unexplainable outcomes.[3]

Since 1948, there is much talk about the land of Israel and the "occupied territories." The fact is that every time Israel fought in a war, they ended up with more land than they started with. This is similar to ancient times. Today Israel is taking the Promised Land in the same way God told them to take it in the time of Moses, little by little and piece by piece (Exod. 23:30; Deut. 7:22). They were to fight for it, settle, live on it, and then continue the process. Based on Scripture, as the people of Israel increase, we can expect her boundaries to do the same.

> When the Most High gave the nations their inheritance, when He separated the sons of man, He set the boundaries of the peoples according to the number of the sons of Israel.
>
> —DEUTERONOMY 32:8

It is God who sets the boundaries of Israel for His people, according to their numbers. As Jewish immigration has increased, so have the borders of the nation. It is also interesting to note that Israel has never possessed all of the land promised to Abraham, Isaac, and Jacob. The tribe of Dan is the only tribe to never receive any of their inheritance, which covers part of present-day Lebanon and Syria. If the Word of God is accurate and the promises of God are true, then this too will come to pass, and we should not be surprised when it does. As the Jewish population increases and tensions rise, we can expect more Israeli wars that will take more land to the north, regardless of world opinion. This is not about a pro-Israel/anti-Arab endorsement of military action but what I believe to be a simple fact of biblical prophecy. Perhaps in the Lord's mercy this expansion will come to pass without a war...but it *will* come to pass because of the faithfulness of God.

I have stated it over and over in this book, but it is worth repeating: the God of the Bible is faithful and is watching over His ancient promises to His people Israel. We have the honor and privilege of watching ancient prophecies being fulfilled in our day. As believers in the Lord Jesus, we no longer need to only watch, but we can also be included in these covenant promises and help bring other promises to pass. Many difficult days are still ahead for Israel, and God is offering us the opportunity as believers to stand with the people He has chosen. One thing is sure: Israel's help is in the name of the Lord, who made heaven and the earth.

> "Had it not been the LORD who was on our side," let Israel now say, "Had it not been the LORD who was on our side when men rose up against us, then they would have swallowed us alive, when their anger was kindled against us; then the waters would have engulfed us, the stream would have swept over our soul; then the raging waters would have swept over our soul." Blessed be the LORD, who has not given us to be torn by their teeth. Our soul has escaped as a bird out of the snare of the trapper; the snare is broken and we have escaped. Our help is in the name of the LORD, who made heaven and earth.
>
> —PSALM 124

Chapter 15

UNIQUE FACTS ABOUT ISRAEL

ISRAEL HAS ACCOMPLISHED in its first sixty years what some nations have not achieved in centuries. These are just a few amazing facts that have come from the present-day nation that is covenanted to God.

Israel, the hundredth-smallest country, with less than 1/1000th of the world's population, can make claim to the following:[1]

NATIONAL

+ Israel is the only liberal democracy in the Middle East.

+ Israel has the world's second-highest per capita of new books.

+ Israel has more museums per capita than any other country.

+ Israel has two official languages: Hebrew and Arabic.

+ Israel has the highest ratio of university degrees to the population in the world.

+ Israel has the highest percentage in the world of home computers per capita.

+ Israel has the third-highest rate of entrepreneurship and the highest rate among women and among people over fifty-five in the world.

+ Relative to its population, Israel is the largest immigrant-absorbing nation on the earth. Immigrants come in search of democracy, religious freedom, and economic opportunity.

ECONOMY

+ Israel is ranked #2 in the world for venture-capital funds, right behind the United States.

+ Israel has the highest average living standards in the Middle East.

+ The per-capita income in 2000 was over $17,500, exceeding that of the United Kingdom.

+ Israel's $100 billion economy is larger than all of its immediate neighbors combined.

+ Outside the United States and Canada, Israel has the largest number of NASDAQ-listed companies.

PEOPLE AND LEADERS

+ Twenty-four percent of Israel's workforce holds university degrees—ranking Israel third in the industrialized world, after the United States and Holland—and 12 percent hold advanced degrees.

+ Israel leads the world in the number of scientists and technicians in the workforce, with 145 per 10,000, as opposed to 85 in the United States, over 70 in Japan, and less than 60 in Germany.

+ With more than 25 percent of its workforce employed in technical professions, Israel places first in this category as well.

+ When Golda Meir was elected prime minister of Israel in 1969, she became the world's second elected female leader in modern times.

+ Professor Robert Aumann is the fourth Israeli in the last four years to win a Nobel Prize.

HUMANITARIAN

+ When the US Embassy in Nairobi, Kenya, was bombed in 1998, Israeli rescue teams were on the scene within a day and saved three victims from the rubble.

+ In 1984 and 1991, Israel airlifted a total of 22,000 Ethiopian Jews at risk in Ethiopia to safety in Israel.

‹ An Israeli company—Patus Ltd.—has donated thousands
of its OdorScreen olfactory gel products to counter the crip-
pling odors faced by on-scene tsunami disaster workers.

‹ Between 150 and 200 multinational clinical trials are regularly taking place in Israel.

‹ Israel was the first nation in the world to adopt the Kimberly
Process, an international standard that certifies diamonds as
"conflict free."

SOCIETY

‹ An Israeli company is providing the technology behind an
American all-electric bus for urban use.

‹ An Israeli company has developed a nano-lubricant that one
day could mean the end of changing your car oil.

‹ An Israeli company was the first to develop and install a
large-scale solar-powered and fully functional electricity gen-
erating plant in Southern California's Mojave Desert.

ENVIRONMENTAL

‹ An Israeli ornithologist is utilizing barn owls to rid large
cities of rodent problems.

‹ Some 500 million birds representing 300 species migrate
across Israel's skies twice a year in the autumn and spring
along the Great Valley Rift.

‹ Israel has the largest raptor migration in the world, with
hundreds of thousands of African birds of prey crossing as
they fan out into Asia.

‹ In response to serious water shortages, Israeli engineers and
agriculturalists developed a revolutionary drip irrigation
system to minimize the amount of water used to grow crops.

‹ An Israeli company has developed sensors that pick up signs
of stress in plants.

+ Israeli biologists have successfully managed, for the first time, to prepare the flowering of the "Madonna Lily"—a rare white Easter lily—in time for Easter.

+ An Israeli company has developed the world's first jellyfish repellent.

+ Israel is the only country in the world that entered the twenty-first century with a net gain in its number of trees. This is even more remarkable since this was achieved in an area considered mainly desert.

+ An Israeli company, Evogene, is developing cotton plants that are resistant to adverse salinity conditions and drought.

+ Israel is one of the leading countries providing ornamental fish to aquariums around the world.

+ Israel annually exports more than 1.5 billion flowers to the United States and Europe.

Military/Security

+ Israel has the fourth-largest air force in the world (after the United States, Russia, and China). In addition to a large variety of other aircraft, Israel's air force has an aerial arsenal of over 250 F-16's. This is the largest fleet of F-16 aircraft outside of the United States.

+ The new American state-of-the-art F-35 Joint Strike Fighter aircraft will be equipped with Israeli-developed mounted display systems in their helmets, which incorporate and display all vital flight data.

+ AirTrain JFK, the 8.1-mile light-rail labyrinth that connects JFK Airport to New York City's mass transit, is protected by the Israeli-developed Nextiva surveillance system.

+ Israel designed the first flight system to protect passenger and freighter aircraft against missile attack.

+ According to industry officials, Israel designed the airline industry's most impenetrable flight security. US officials now look to Israel for advice on how to handle airborne security threats.

+ Israeli-developed security precautions have been adopted in Maryland and Washington.

+ Israeli researchers have developed an engineless nano-RPV (remote piloted vehicle).

MEDICAL ADVANCEMENTS

+ A portable electrocardiograph machine developed by Israeli company SHL can transmit highly detailed data on heart activity to physicians by mobile phone.

+ Israeli start-up Audiodent has developed an innovative hearing aid that clips easily inside the mouth, using the teeth and jawbone to transmit sound to the brain.

+ Israeli researchers have discovered the molecular trigger that causes psoriasis.

+ An Israeli scientific team from Technion has succeeded in creating beating heart tissue from human embryonic stem cells in the laboratory.

+ An Israeli company has unveiled a blood test that, via the telephone, diagnoses heart attacks.

+ Israeli researchers have created a "biological pacemaker" that corrects faulty heart rhythms when injected into the failing hearts of pigs.

+ An Israeli company has developed a device that helps nurses locate hard to find veins.

+ An Israeli company has developed a simple blood test that distinguishes between mild and more severe cases of multiple sclerosis.

+ Israel's Given Imaging developed the first ingestible video camera, so small it fits inside a pill. Used to view the small intestine from the inside, the camera helps doctors diagnose cancer and digestive disorders. More than 65,000 patients worldwide have swallowed the M2A capsule.

+ Israeli medical researchers have shown that lycopene, the red pigment found in tomatoes, lowers blood pressure.

+ Israeli researchers have shown that a daily dosage of vitamin E is effective in helping to regain hearing loss.

+ An Israeli invented a "bone glue" that will reduce the need for bone transplants and heal bone defects caused by cancer, and that respectively stimulates speedy bone and cartilage repair and enables faster and improved healing of injuries.

DISEASE RESEARCH

+ Israeli scientists have alleviated Parkinson's-like symptoms in rats.

+ The Israeli-developed Ex-Press shunt is providing relief for American glaucoma sufferers.

+ An Israeli research team has found that the combination of electrical stimulation and chemotherapy makes cancerous metastases disappear.

+ Israeli scientists developed the first fully computerized, no-radiation diagnostic instrumentation for breast cancer.

+ Israeli researchers are using video games to investigate future treatments for memory disorders such as Alzheimer's disease.

+ A team of Israeli genetic researchers has identified a genetic defect that causes a severe neurodegenerative disease in Bedouin children, resulting in premature death.

+ A team from the Weizmann Institute has demonstrated for the first time how tissues transplanted from pig embryos might, in the future, be able to induce the human body to produce blood-clotting proteins for hemophilia patients.

+ Two Israelis have won the 2004 Nobel Prize for Chemistry for their groundbreaking work in cancer research.

+ Israeli scientists have created a DNA nano-computer that not only detects cancer but also releases drugs to treat the disease.

+ The Weizmann Institute of Science has been voted the best university in the world for life scientists to conduct research.

MEDICINE/VACCINES

+ Israeli microbiologists have developed the first passive vaccine against the mosquito-borne West Nile virus.

+ An Israeli company has been given a US grant to develop an anti-smallpox first-aid-treatment kit.

+ Israeli scientists are developing a nose drop that will provide a five-year flu vaccine.

+ An Israeli-developed elderberry extract is one of America's best-selling flu prevention medicines.

+ Israeli research has found that citrus oils may hold the key for asthma treatment.

+ An Israeli company has developed a device that could enable millions of American diabetics to painlessly inject themselves with insulin.

+ Israeli researchers have discovered a new way to create effective substitutes for antibiotics, based on a combination of amino acids and fatty acids.

+ An Israeli-developed device can painlessly administer medications through microscopic pores in the skin.

+ Israeli researchers are successfully using magnets to treat post-traumatic stress disorder.

+ An Israeli doctor headed the Merck team that developed a vaccine against cervical cancer.

Cosmetic

+ Israeli company Ultrashape has developed a safe replacement for liposuction: a unique new body-contouring device that "blasts" unwanted fat from the body.

+ An Israeli FDA-approved device, the VelaSmooth, reduces the appearance of cellulite.

+ Israeli laser technology is powering the latest hair removal devices on the American market.

+ A new acne treatment developed in Israel, the ClearLight device, produces a high-intensity, ultraviolet light—a free, narrow-band blue light that causes acne bacteria to self-destruct, all without damaging surrounding skin or tissue.

Technology

+ The cell phone was developed in Israel by Israelis working in the Israeli branch of Motorola, which has its largest development center in Israel.

+ An Israeli company has developed the world's first video ringtones for cell pones, the Vringo.

+ Voice-over internet protocol (VoIP) technology was pioneered in Israel.

+ Intel's new multi-core processor was completely developed at its facilities in Israel.

+ Most of the Windows NT operating system was developed by Microsoft-Israel.

+ The first PC anti-virus software was developed in Israel in 1979.

+ The Israeli company M-Systems was the first to patent and introduce key chain storage.

+ The Pentium MMX Chip technology was designed in Israel at Intel.

+ Voice mail technology was developed in Israel.

+ The technology for AOL Instant Messenger was developed in 1996 by four young Israelis.

+ Research by three scientists from the Haifa Technion made the transmission of video pictures from Mars by the NASA explorer "Spirit" possible thanks to a unique algorithm developed by Technion graduates.

+ A small Israel company, called Lenslet, has developed a revolutionary electro-optic processor, which operates one thousand times faster than any known digital signal processor.

+ Israeli engineers are behind the development of the largest communications router in the world, launched by Cisco.

RESEARCH/DEVELOPMENT

+ Israel produces more scientific papers per capita than any other nation by a large margin—109 per 10,000 people—as well as one of the highest per-capita rates of patents filed.

+ In proportion to its population, Israel has the largest number of start-up companies in the world. In absolute terms, Israel has the largest number of start-up companies than any other country in the world, except the United States (3,500 companies, mostly in hi-tech).

+ Israeli research shows that we can find out more about what is buried beneath the earth's surface by launching a satellite into the sky.

+ With more than three thousand high-tech companies and start-ups, Israel has the highest concentration of hi-tech companies in the world (apart from the Silicon Valley).

+ Both Microsoft and Cisco built their only R&D facilities outside the United States in Israel.

+ Motorola has its largest R&D center outside of the United States in Israel.

+ Israel hosts IBM's largest R&D facilities outside the United States.

- ◆ A team of Israeli and US researchers have designed a watermelon-picking robot endowed with artificial vision to do the job of harvesting.

- ◆ Scientists in Israel have used strands of DNA to create tiny transistors that can literally build themselves.

- ◆ On a per-capita basis, Israel has the largest number of biotech start-ups.

All the above has happened while engaged in regular wars with an implacable enemy that seeks its destruction, while facing continual economic strain from spending more per capita on its own protection than any other country on Earth.

At the writing of this book, more and more amazing discoveries and achievements are coming from the land of Israel in many different fields of study and research. In the future, because of God's love and everlasting promises, we can expect many more.

Behold, He who keeps Israel will neither slumber nor sleep.

—PSALM 121:4

HOW to PRAY for ISRAEL:
THE ISAIAH 62 PRAYER GUIDE

P SALM 122:6 TELLS us to pray for the peace of Jerusalem, yet when the call
is made to pray, many Christians feel confused and do not know where
to begin.

Hopefully after reading this book, that is no longer the case for you. My
desire is that you will take all that you have learned in these pages and turn it
toward heaven with a more focused intercession. Understanding God's purpose toward Israel is not enough to see His plans unfold. Daniel 11:32 says
that "the people who know their God will display strength and take action."
Through prayer, God has given us an invitation to enter into the ongoing
fulfillment of the Old and New Testament promises regarding Israel. If you
are a Christian, this includes you. God's original desire for Israel has never
changed since He said, "I will also walk among you and be your God, and you
shall be My people" (Lev. 26:12).

The best way to begin is by praying the Word of God and reminding the
Lord of what He has said. We will use Isaiah 62 as our prayer guide. Start by
reading Isaiah 62 out loud, beginning to end. Then, with your heart turned
toward the Father, go back and start to pray as the Holy Spirit leads you,
using the scriptures in Isaiah 62 to focus on specific aspects of Israel.

To help you get started, I have separated Isaiah 62 into seven portions,
with suggested prayer points and references to previous chapters in this book
to guide your understanding. Just as Isaiah 62:7 says, "Give Him no rest until
He establishes and makes Jerusalem a praise in the earth"!

Isaiah 62:1

> For Zion's sake I will not keep silent, and for Jerusalem's sake I
> will not keep quiet, until her righteousness goes forth like bright-
> ness, and her salvation like a torch that is burning.

Pray for God's heart for Israel within the church, that the things on His
heart would be on your heart and that you would be motivated to pray and

take action and not to be silent. (Read the Introduction, "Why Care about Israel?")

Pray that Israel's true righteousness, salvation, and peace (Jesus) would shine forth brightly from Jerusalem. (Read chapter 3, "Peace.")

Pray that Jerusalem will become all that God intended it to be as a place where He establishes His name and gathers His people to Himself. (Read chapter 12, "The Value of Jerusalem.")

Isaiah 62:2–3

> The nations will see your righteousness, and all kings your glory; and you will be called by a new name which the mouth of the Lord will designate. You will also be a crown of beauty in the hand of the Lord, and a royal diadem in the hand of your God.

Pray that the nations will see the favor of God on present-day Israel and all He has done through her and that the nations will be drawn to God. (Read chapter 15, "Unique Facts About Israel.")

Pray that the kings, presidents, and prime ministers of the earth will recognize now that those who bless Israel will be blessed. (Read chapter 2, "Blessings and Curses.")

Pray that Israel will step into her destiny as a royal diadem and a holy people, as God intended. (Read chapter 1, "The Chosen People.")

Isaiah 62:4

> It will no longer be said to you, "Forsaken," nor to your land will it any longer be said, "Desolate"; but you will be called, "My delight is in her," and your land, "Married"; for the Lord delights in you, and to Him your land will be married.

Repent of how the church has called Israel "desolate" and "forsaken." If needed, repent of any anti-Semitism or personal rejection of Israel you've carried in your own heart, such as a rejection of God's plan and choice. (Read chapter 5, "Has God Rejected Israel?")

Proclaim that God's delight is in the land of Israel and with the Jewish people and that He has not forsaken Israel or His covenant with her. (Read chapter 6, "Blessings of the Jews.")

Pray that the church will recognize her Jewish roots and not be arrogant toward the "natural branches" that were broken off. Pray that the "natural branches" will soon be restored in unity through the Messiah, both Jew and Gentile, as one in God's olive tree. (Read chapter 7, "Christians Grafted In.")

Isaiah 62:5

> For as a young man marries a virgin, so your sons will marry you; and as the bridegroom rejoices over the bride, so your God will rejoice over you.

Pray that Israelis will have a revelation of who they are in God's plan and join themselves and be committed to the land of Israel. (Read chapter 6, "Blessings of the Jews.")

Pray that Israeli nationalism will be strong and unified as God is fulfilling Scripture by gathering together the outcasts of Israel to rejoice over them and reveal Himself to them. (Read chapter 13, "Making *Aliyah*.")

Pray that the Jewish nation will see that a wedding celebration with God is coming to Jerusalem and that the Bridegroom, Jesus, the Jewish Messiah, is coming for them again! (Read chapter 8, "Importance of Feasts.")

Isaiah 62:6–7

> On your walls, O Jerusalem, I have appointed watchmen; all day and all night they will never keep silent. You who remind the LORD, take no rest for yourselves; and give Him no rest until He establishes and makes Jerusalem a praise in the earth.

Pray that God will continue to raise up "watchmen" and those concerned for Israel's physical and spiritual condition (Ps. 102:13–17) to pray and not keep silent before the Lord concerning Israel. Pray that those who are praying for the nation of Israel would not grow weary in their prayers and intercession to God. (Read the introduction, "Why Care About Israel?")

Pray that God would truly establish present-day Jerusalem as a praise and a wonder in all the earth and that the nations of the earth would look toward Jerusalem and see the Lord dwelling in the place He has chosen to establish His name. (Read chapter 12, "The Value of Jerusalem.")

Isaiah 62:8–9

> The Lord has sworn by His right hand and by His strong arm, "I will never again give your grain as food for your enemies; nor will foreigners drink your new wine for which you have labored." But those who garner it will eat it and praise the Lord; and those who gather it will drink it in the courts of My sanctuary.

Pray that God would be Israel's defense and protection in the days ahead and that the land that God promised to Israel will be theirs. (Read chapter 14, "Israel Today.")

Pray that God would curse those who are cursing Israel and confuse enemy plans to destroy Israel and steal her labors and what has God has given her. Pray that these nations would turn from their curses and receive the true peace of God. (Read chapter 2, "Blessings and Curses," and chapter 3, "Peace.")

Pray that Israelis would recognize God's protection and defense of Israel and give praise to the Lord and trust in Him. (Read chapter 14, "Israel Today.")

Isaiah 62:10–12

> Go through, go through the gates, clear the way for the people; build up, build up the highway, remove the stones, lift up a standard over the peoples. Behold, the Lord has proclaimed to the end of the earth, say to the daughter of Zion, "Lo, your salvation comes; behold His reward is with Him, and His recompense before Him." And they will call them, "The holy people, the redeemed of the Lord"; and you will be called, "Sought out, a city not forsaken."

Pray that the present-day nation of Israel will be seen as an instrument of God and a demonstration of God's faithfulness to the people of the earth. (Read chapter 15, "Unique Facts About Israel.")

Proclaim with the Lord to the ends of the earth, and especially to the "daughter of Zion": "Your salvation *has* come! His reward is with Him!" Pray for the salvation of all of Israel and that Israel with enter into the new covenant that Jeremiah 31:31 speaks of and that they will all know the Lord. (Read chapter 7, "Christians Grafted In.")

Pray for the Messianic believers and congregations in Israel to continue to grow in strength, faith, and love in the Messiah and that they may have the passion for the Son of God and the fire of the Holy Spirit that their first-century brethren had. (Read chapter 4, "Jesus and the Law.")

For those of you who have prayed or are praying for Israel:

> The LORD bless you from Zion, and may you see the prosperity of Jerusalem all the days of your life. Indeed, may you see your children's children. Peace be upon Israel!
>
> —PSALM 128:5–6

NOTES

CHAPTER 4

1. *Why Israel?* (Teaching CD, track 1, 2:15) © 1998 Derek Prince Ministries.

CHAPTER 9

1. Ray Vander Laan, *Echoes of His Presence* (Grand Rapids, MI: Zondervan, 1996), 147.

CHAPTER 11

1. Alfred Edersheim, *The Temple: Its Ministry and Services*, updated ed. (Peabody, MA: Hendrickson Publishers, 1994), 227.
2. Ibid.
3. Ibid., 221.

CHAPTER 13

1. From website: http://jppi.org.il/uploads/Jewish%20Demography.pdf (accessed February 14, 2011).

CHAPTER 14

1. Mark Twain, *The Innocents Abroad, or The New Pilgrim's Progress* (New York: The Modern Library, Random House, 2003).
2. *Against All Odds* (DVD series), episode 6: "The Miracle of '48" © 2006 American Trademark Pictures, LLC.
3. Ibid., and from website: www.againstalloddstv.com/miracles.php, "The national miracle of Israel" (accessed February 16, 2011).

CHAPTER 15

1. Facts reprinted with permission from ISRAEL21c (www.israel21c.org).

ABOUT the AUTHOR

DOUG HERSHEY AND his wife, Rebecca, are the directors of The Ebed Network, based in southern Maine. Their vision for The Ebed Network is to teach biblical foundations of the New Covenant through the Jewish perspective of the scriptures, as well as to provide various opportunities to bless Israel in practical ways, according to Romans 15:25–27. Doug and Rebecca have traveled extensively, including to Israel, and currently live in southern Maine with their four children, Elijah, Josiah, Levi, and Rachel.

Additional information can be found at www.EbedNetwork.com.

CONTACT the AUTHOR

Additional information can be found at www.EbedNetwork.com.